13 MONTHS

IN THE BUSH, IN VIETNAM, IN 1968.

BRUCE A. BASTIEN

Thirteen Months
My Vietnam War

Copyright © 2020 Bruce A. Bastien.

All rights reserved. No part of this book may be used or reproduced by any means, graphic, electronic, or mechanical, including photocopying, recording, taping or by any information storage retrieval system without the written permission of the author except in the case of brief quotations embodied in critical articles and reviews.

iUniverse books may be ordered through booksellers or by contacting:

iUniverse
1663 Liberty Drive
Bloomington, IN 47403
www.iuniverse.com
844-349-9409

Because of the dynamic nature of the Internet, any web addresses or links contained in this book may have changed since publication and may no longer be valid. The views expressed in this work are solely those of the author and do not necessarily reflect the views of the publisher, and the publisher hereby disclaims any responsibility for them.

Any people depicted in stock imagery provided by Getty Images are models, and such images are being used for illustrative purposes only.
Certain stock imagery © Getty Images.

ISBN: 978-1-6632-0456-1 (sc)
ISBN: 978-1-6632-0458-5 (hc)
ISBN: 978-1-6632-0457-8 (e)

Library of Congress Control Number: 2020911935

Print information available on the last page.

iUniverse rev. date: 01/27/2021

CONTENTS

Acknowledgments v
Book Reviews vii
Introduction ix

Chapter 1   Hallucinations 1
Chapter 2   Operation Allen Brook 3
Chapter 3   Facing the Dragon 19
Chapter 4   On Operation 25
Chapter 5   Beginnings 35
Chapter 6   Arrival 41
Chapter 7   The 3/5 Battalion Area 47
Chapter 8   Anderson Bridge 61
Chapter 9   The Old French Fort 67
Chapter 10   Mountain Operations 77
Chapter 11   Lang Co 87
Chapter 12   Phu Bai 97
Chapter 13   Operation Mameluke Thrust 107
Chapter 14   Operation Meade River 119
Chapter 15   Going Home 133
Chapter 16   Aftermath 139

Glossary 145
About the Author 149

ACKNOWLEDGMENTS

I would like to acknowledge the following individuals who have helped make this memoir possible. Without their insight, expertise, reviews, and encouragement, I never would have completed this book.

Neil Brodin, friend and former army soldier

Ernie Burciaga, friend and former Vietnam army soldier

Dave Feehan, friend and author

Ron Heath, friend and former Vietnam marine, author contributor

Rick Maddy, friend and former Vietnam marine, author contributor

Ron McCarville, friend and former Vietnam marine, author contributor

Christy Sauro, friend and former Vietnam marine, author of *The Twins Platoon*

Fred Smith, friend and former Vietnam marine, picture contributor, Kilo Company commander

Editors at iUniverse, who were all more than helpful and encouraging

BOOK REVIEWS

Bruce Bastien's 13 Months in Vietnam overlapped my tour in 1968 when we served together in 3rd Battalion 5th Marines. This period marked the highest casualty rates of the war, and he lays out perfectly the incongruous mix of hard duty, boredom, humor, characters, comradery, fear, danger, and lethal fighting that marked our time there. Bruce was a fine Marine, but it's clear he's also an exceptional writer.

-Frederick W. Smith, Chairman & CEO FedEx

This is a personal account of the, feelings, frustration, horror and friendships, of a young man under very exceptional conditions. It describes the grassroot experiences of a young marine on a mission for his country, but where questions arise of the ultimate purpose, the Why. It is not a story of heroes, but a sincere description of what a young American boy experienced. What was the purpose of this war? And even, what was the purpose of some of the movements of the soldier's unit? This is a very realistic story of how many young Americans must have experienced their role in Vietnam. The narrative doesn't dwell in excesses, or drama, yet describes the horror and fright very clearly, but also the extreme boredom and man-to-man conflicts that arose. Altogether, the story is told in a very compact way with plenty of photographs, which help the reader to become part of the story. This is one of the best personal descriptions of the Vietnam war that I have read, probably because it is so realistic and well written. At the end it also includes musings by the Author about the meaning of it all. Very readable stuff!

-Mårten Wikström, Helsinki, Finland

"13 Months" is a valuable and necessary read to give people who never served "in country," a rare, unheroic, but brutally true picture of what the Vietnam experience was really like. Thank you Bruce, I now understand!

-Neil Brodin, former Army soldier and career Policeman

Those of us who were old enough to remember the war in Vietnam either served in the military or protested against the war; but in either case, Bruce Bastien gives the reader an extremely realistic, compelling description. of the violence, the boredom, the camaraderie, and the frustrations that a marine "grunt" experienced during his 13 month tour of duty. Bruce faced the question of life or death on almost a daily basis. and yet, he approached this as having a "job to do," and he did it as well as anyone could in his shoes. This book is must reading for those who went and those who did not. This was a war we should never forget.

-Dave Feehan, CEO Civitas Consultants

I just finished reading "13 Months". It was entertaining, engaging, and enlightening and I felt true emotions in every chapter. You don't get a sense of the realness of a time/situation in history books like you do with a first-hand account.

-Tonia Senoo

The book was fantastic. It bought back so many memories. I returned to Vietnam FOUR years ago and it's exactly as the author thought it would be. It's built up with paved roads, not at all like it was in 67 68. I did get a chance to visit An HOA on my return trip and I couldn't recognize anything. In fact, I was standing on the airstrip and didn't know it until a former marine helicopter pilot rode up on a motorcycle and told me I was standing on the airstrip. This was one of the best books I've read about Vietnam. Everything I read was a hundred percent accurate.

-Amazon Kindle Customer

I was 30 years old, married with two preschoolers, in 1968 when Bruce Bastien spent 13 months in the bush, in Vietnam.

The war sickened me. I had no stomach for protest marching. My only priority was to prevent my children from ever seeing the carnage on television.

Bruce writes the way he talks, and his voice holds the story together. His sense of humor, coupled with no-holds-barred graphic descriptions and Marine Corps language, makes 13 Months one of the most shattering, page-turning stories I've ever read. Yet many passages of his story show deep respect for the land and village people of Vietnam. Bonds between the young men who served together in Kilo 3/5 Unit squad (Third Battalion Fifth Marines) will never be forgotten. Though not a fan of books about war, I could not put this book down.

-Kathy Hughart

INTRODUCTION

One day in 1997, I came across an email from a guy named Ron Heath, who said he was looking for Bruce Bastien, who had been a marine in Vietnam with him in 1968. I scratched my head and had to think for a minute or two. After all, it had been over thirty years and I hadn't really thought about it much since then.

Ron Heath, Ron Heath ... Whoa, I did remember him! He was that pack rat guy who carried an almost complete NVA (North Vietnamese Army) uniform, gear, and weapons with him until bringing most of it home. We exchanged several emails wherein he explained that he was trying to contact as many guys as possible from our time there. He wanted to start a website where we could all post our stories and keep in touch. His goal was to collect our memories, while we still had some, so we'd always have them available.

For the next few years, he continued that quest and as time went by we collected several stories from different people. We even had a reunion or two. The website grew and became popular. But times and fortunes change and Ron became unable to maintain the site. No one in our group had the ability to maintain a website, and it gradually became old and outdated. The code behind the website finally became so obsolete that it couldn't even be migrated to the newer platforms or newer software.

As it became obvious the website was not salvageable, I decided to write my own story about my time in Vietnam. I wanted to include in my memoir a few of the most cogent and touching stories by a few of the other guys from the website in order to keep them alive and to tell our true stories, as best we could, as we had lived them.

These are all firsthand, first-person, personal stories told by the people who lived them. They are as real and true as our memories allow. Some will contain death, near death, injury, and fear. Some will contain the boredom, tediousness, and simple unpleasantness of a long year spent in Vietnam. Some will relate the strange and funny things that happened along the way.

These insider stories are our attempt to let you see how it was, what it was, and to experience in some small part the emotions that we all felt. But mostly it is a personal story of my thirteen months in Vietnam—the good, the bad, and the ugly, as I remember it.

There is not enough time, space, or energy available to repeat all the stories, all the names, all the events, or all the emotions. I apologize for the stories not included from the website and the names not mentioned, but please know that the men of Kilo 3/5 (that would be Kilo Company, Third Battalion, Fifth Marines) who were in Vietnam were and are dedicated Americans who did the jobs they were sent to do, despite the fear and the danger.

This is also a story of happenstance and the roles luck and chance play in determining who lives or dies, who gets wounded, and who skates through hazardous events unscathed and unharmed.

I obviously succeeded in surviving my entire thirteen months in Vietnam, meaning that I was never killed, wounded, or medevacked because of illness or injury. I did my job and what was asked—no more, no less. Certainly, I was nothing special and did nothing particularly heroic, but I was there and I served and supported. This is a story of personal growth and learning about friendship, love, difficulties, danger, deprivation, and loss.

The Vietnam experience is one that never leaves you completely. In one way or another, it affects the rest of your days. It lives inside, sometimes deeply hidden and sometimes just below the surface, but it is always waiting and wanting to get out.

In my case, I came back healthy and whole. I was not scarred physically or emotionally, at least on the surface. I was able to continue with a "normal" life. However, after writing this memoir, I have discovered feelings and emotions that seemed almost nonexistent before. I am now more aware than ever of that entire episode. I feel sadness at the destruction and loss. It can't be undone, but writing about it at least has helped release the emotional turmoil from decades ago. I have tried to express it in these stories.

THIRTEEN MONTHS

CHAPTER 1

HALLUCINATIONS

It was late May 1968, a hot time of the year in Vietnam. My unit, Kilo 3/5 of the USMC, was tramping to Go Noi Island to replace another embattled battalion. I was now hallucinating. The extreme heat and the torturous long walk into the bush had worn us down to the breaking point. I was standing on a small island of tall elephant grass in a dry, sandy riverbed. The grass stood well above my head and blocked even the slightest breeze from flowing through. I was having trouble breathing the hot, humid, still air in that stifling oven. A ferocious sun beat down on us as if we were pork links under the broiler. I thought I'd pass out if we didn't start moving again soon. When I could see down the dry riverbed, I noticed that the white-hot sand was shimmering and dancing as the superheated air above it rose in wavy patterns.

We had already been walking five or six hours, along either Highway 1 or one of the other routes, down from Hill 55 near Da Nang. I don't remember which road it was. They had rousted us out of our sleeping holes at oh dark thirty in the early morning, and we were told, "Saddle up. We're moving out."

It doesn't take long to "saddle up" when you've been sleeping on the ground in your clothes, wearing your boots, and all your gear has been packed tight waiting right next to you. So we got up and strapped on the backpacks, weapons and ammo, and everything else we owned. Off we went down the road. None of us grunts knew where we were going, but that was nothing new.

Stopped in the elephant grass, the sixty- or seventy-pound load on my back was cutting painfully into my shoulders. While we had been walking, I could kind of bounce the pack up and down with each step, temporarily getting the weight off one shoulder and then off the other. Just standing there not moving, it hung like deadweight, with no relief. I endured the pain but felt myself losing it in the lethal heat.

I must have been a sight—the round steel hardhat helmet sat askew on my head because of the mail received from home stuffed up in the helmet liner for safekeeping. It had a chin strap hanging down one side uselessly. My metal military-issue glasses were held away from my nose with bits of cardboard to keep the lenses from steaming up in the hot, humid air. My green T-shirt under the open flak jacket vest was a dark and sweaty black because the vest prevented sweat from evaporating. Stinging, salty sweat rolled down my face into my eyes, and my back was hot and itchy.

The utility belt around my waist had three hanging canteens of water, mostly empty already, and a gas mask never used but there just in case. I had a .45-caliber pistol attached at the belt, but I carried no M16 rifle. Instead, I carried the mortar and baseplate on one shoulder or the other, cushioned by my olive-green towel.

Holding all this up were those wonderful rubber-soled brown-and-green canvas–sided jungle boots with the grommet holes in the side so that water could drain out as you walked along after wading through another jungle stream or rice paddy. You could go anywhere in them: rivers, rice paddies, jungles, or even mountains.

The pain in my shoulders was intense. I distinctly remember thinking that those shoulder straps would actually slice all the way through my shoulders and my arms would fall off onto the ground. It hurt so bad I wanted to scream. I wanted to rip the backpack off and just run away.

Instead, I hallucinated as I looked down to where my arms would fall when it happened and daydreamed about what I'd do in that case. There was nowhere to go, and I wouldn't have any arms or hands anyway. I was sure that I'd be easy prey for the bad guys, but I was just too tired to care. The exhaustion and heat had drained me of any rational thought.

Dizzy from the heat and thin, still air, shoulders in pain, and hallucinating about arms falling off onto the ground, it dawned on me as I squirmed in agony that I was visualizing my dismemberment by my own stupid backpack.

Hey, dumb shit, your arms aren't really falling off onto the ground. It just feels that way, I heard myself thinking as I fought to get out of my stupor.

I had heard the sounds of the firefight up ahead about a quarter mile away, so I knew why we had stopped. We were to stop our march to Go Noi Island when we arrived, and we would know that we had arrived when we found the tree line, the one lined with the North Vietnamese Army.

I should have gotten down, but the sand was just too hot and I was just too tired. I stood and waited for it to be over so we could press on. I waited and waited. The fatigue and pain had caused me to not even think about or care about ever getting home again. It caused me to abandon taking any precautions. I wasn't thinking about chance or luck any more. I really wasn't thinking at all. I just stood and waited, daydreaming and hallucinating in and out of reality. What would be would be.

Finally, I heard the swish and roar of the jets and the five-hundred-pound bomb explosions. They made several passes. I hoped and prayed that meant we'd be moving again soon. And actually, shortly thereafter we were moving. My short excursion into insanity was over for the day, at least for the while—or so I hoped.

Moving again, I began thinking about the possibilities. It seemed more and more likely that if the bad guys didn't get us, the environment would. Even without an army of hostiles trying to kill us, this brutal land was trying its best to see that we didn't ever go home.

This is just too extreme, too intense, too hard, I thought. *Nobody can do this, nor should they even try.* Yet here we were once again. Where we were going and what we'd find when we got there was still unknown. However, since this was only our first skirmish of the day, and the day was young, I was sure there would be more to come.

CHAPTER 2

OPERATION ALLEN BROOK

We were moving again, but I was already dreading the next encounter as we trudged forward on the hot, dry riverbed. I watched as the marines ahead of me turned right and disappeared, one after the other, into the jungle forest. It was slow going now, single file. Keep your spacing and don't clusterfuck. The heat and humidity remained unabated. It was painfully slow and excruciatingly uncomfortable. The first round of skirmishes had passed, and we cleared that hurdle using jets and bombs, but another could come at any moment. I had been here six months already, and I had seen Tet come and go. We didn't know it then, but we were being brought in to stop the new "Mini-Tet" offensive by the NVA.

The Third Battalion, Fifth Marine Regiment had arrived. We had crossed into Go Noi Island territory past Liberty Bridge, which had already been blown up by the NVA. We were officially on Operation Allen Brook. It was late May of 1968.

From then on, we swept, searched, and destroyed. We looked to contact the enemy, and when it was made, we engaged, fought, and called in artillery or air strikes until they were killed or retreated—and then we pressed on and did it all over again. We covered the same territory again and again. This might go on for weeks. We did not know. In fact, we didn't know what later that day would bring, let alone how long this would last.

Our goal was to eradicate the Vietcong and NVA from this entire area. Go Noi was considered a safe haven for the NVA infiltrating from Laos, and it was used to launch rocket attacks into Da Nang. Defending Da Nang from rocket attack was our main responsibility. Operation Allen Brook combined several marine battalions into search and destroy missions to remove enemies from the area. We would encounter NVA soldiers and local units of the Vietcong. This was a very hostile area, and fighting would be intense.

The entire region was located just north of the Que Son Mountains, which ran east and west to Laos, and provided a route for infiltration into the Da Nang area from the south. The mountains were heavily forested, canopied, and filled with all sorts of beautiful birds, monkeys, snakes, insects, streams, and waterfalls. There were sometimes bears and even an occasional tiger or boar.

Go Noi Island (part of the mainland and not really an island) was flat and crisscrossed with rivers and streams flowing down from the mountains to the sea through jungles, rice paddies, and open fields. Some of the small streams were dry now in this hot season, but larger streams and rivers still had running water, some of it quite deep. It usually rained heavily around sunset and sometimes well into the night. We crossed rivers and streams daily, and we were rained on at night. We couldn't keep dry, and foot rot was a problem. We were either hot and dry or wet and cold. Temperatures had been reported as 115 degrees or higher during the day, and the humidity seemed as high. It was nasty hot, and heat stroke was always a danger. You had to keep hydrated.

The operation actually started May 4, 1968, and it would ultimately continue to the end of August 1968. For us, it was taking place in an area about ten to fifteen miles south of Da Nang and five miles east of An Hoa, with the South China Sea to the east. It was a big box of land.

By most accounts, Operation Allen Brook at Go Noi Island was a series of some of the most brutal battles of the Vietnam War. The whole area was named "Dodge City" by marines because of the frequent shootouts and ambushes. It was also called "Arizona Territory."

There had been previous operations in this area to clean it out. Not maintaining a permanent presence allowed Charlie to re-infiltrate, resupply, and rebuild. Then we had to clear it again. I'm not sure why that was allowed. It was just a fact of this war and a decision made by top leadership.

Originally, the Third Battalion, Twenty-Seventh Marines, and the Seventh Marines were first into the region. They ran into an NVA Regimental command post and supply depot. Over several days, there was fierce resistance and they were ambushed, mortared, RPG'ed, and machine-gunned as well as hit with the usual AK-47 small arms fire and booby traps. Fighting was horrific. The NVA had been at home here, dug in for the long haul, and fought from trenches, reinforced concrete bunkers, hooches, fighting holes, tunnels, and the villages that they had commandeered.

Marines were ambushed in the fields, rice paddies, riverbeds, gullies, and tall elephant grasses—anywhere they had the least cover. Charlie chose the locations and times. Artillery and mortars weren't able to dislodge him. It took air strikes and ground assaults by the marines to end the resistance. There were many casualties. The marines of 3/7 would later be awarded a Medal of Honor, two Navy Crosses, seven Silver Stars, and the Presidential Unit Citation.

My unit (Kilo Company, Third Battalion, Fifth Marines) along with the rest of the battalion was to replace the Third Battalion, Twenty-Seventh Marines, who had become "combat ineffective" because of casualties and the almost total annihilation of their officers and staff NCO, thus our long walk to Go Noi Island.

But first we had to link up with what was left of 3/27. We'd entered Go Noi Island tense and expectant as we forged ahead to find what was left of them. The Seventh Marines had also been hammered hard but remained functional in their section of Go Noi.

Whether on a company-wide sweep, a platoon-wide sweep, a squad-size patrol, or even a fire team patrol, there would always be a point squad and a point man. The point was responsible for getting us to where we were going. It was the most dangerous and grueling job there was. The point man had to be swapped out frequently because it was such a hellacious task. It was dangerous and hard work. A man became tired and careless quickly. The point was tasked with spotting the ambush and avoiding booby traps while hacking his way through the jungle or while approaching a tree line from the rice paddies.

Sometimes the point walked directly into an enemy ambush. Sometimes the enemy waited hidden along the path until the point was well past and then opened up on the middle. Sometimes the enemy could hear us coming and had time to set booby traps.

Today Second Platoon was point for Kilo Company. They were advancing into the area where we were to meet up with the remainder of 3/27. We would take control where they left off. To link up, Second Platoon had to cut their way through a thick bamboo jungle forest.

It took most of the day to hack through to the clearing on the other side. It was incredibly difficult and slow going to hack through bamboo and thick jungle underbrush with a machete. The point man held the vines and leaves away with his left hand and cut the vines, branches, and leaves with the machete in his right hand. Now that he could see the ground in front of him, he looked to make sure there were no booby traps planted where he would step and that there were no grenades hanging in the next bunch of vines and leaves. He stepped ahead and did it all over again.

He used his left hand to wipe away the sweat rolling down his forehead into his eyes. The heat and humidity were exhausting. Bamboo and vegetation cut and bruised the body. Every muscle ached. The exertion poured stinging, salty, itchy sweat down his neck, onto his back, and across every pore of his body. Insects stung and bit. With every step, there was the possibility he had missed seeing a land mine or a grenade strung in the vines. An ambush could be waiting behind the next bush.

Once through to the other side, the Second Platoon finally met up with the remains of 3/27 and their battle. According to Ron McCarville (Second Platoon squad leader), "Hell happened here."

McCarville compared well to a fire ant, small, brave, aggressive, and unusually strong for his size. He had a stinging voice that commanded attention. McCarville was a guy wired on adrenaline, whether it was from sense of duty or fear in these situations. He was always on duty. He moved fast, decided quickly, and led by example. He was all business. The image I had of him was a man running from fighting hole to fighting hole with his hair on fire, barking orders, and making sure things were done correctly. If you were in Mac's squad, you didn't get any unauthorized rest.

I knew McCarville from last Christmas, when I'd met him at the bottom of a rain-soaked trench after the Battalion Christmas Eve celebration where we had gotten drunk. Later that evening, we had jumped into the same trench because Charlie had mortared the base, wishing us a Merry Christmas. Several of us spent the night in that trench, at the old battalion area, and we were rained on most of the night. At least we had gotten steak and beer before the mortars came in.

As a leader, Mac was always out front commanding the action and doing the things that needed to be done. He never asked anyone to do something he wasn't already doing himself or had not already done before. He was tenacious in finishing the job he set out to do. It didn't matter how nasty the job.

Here, in his own words, McCarville tells us what Second Platoon encountered in meeting up with 3/27:

> The bodies were stacked like cordwood on a sandy creek bottom. We sent a fire team to fill canteens, and they were downstream from the bodies. A stream of crimson fluid had formed on the downhill side of the bodies and was blending with the flow of the stream, turning it a shade of red. We had to send a runner to let them know not to fill the canteens. Screaming didn't work.
>
> 3/27 had met its fate, and many brave marines had died. Their gear was everywhere. There were gobs of blood on the ground, bloody bandages, shell casings, and NVA gear, helmets, and discarded weapons. CH-46 helicopters were choppering marine WIA/KIA out, seemingly nonstop. With every landing or departure, ponchos covering the dead were whipped up and down by the rotor blades, exposing bodies and body parts that had once been 3/27 Marines caught in the killing fields.
>
> I had talked to a corporal from 3/27. He had a blank look on his face and told me, "We assaulted the trench eight times. We were repulsed seven, and then we went hand to hand the eighth time. We took the trench." As he leaned back against the hole he was in, the final elements of the NVA regiment they had walked into were being cleared from some

bunkers within viewing distance. He watched, as I did, and we never said anything else to each other.

I couldn't help but think of WWII and the Pacific. Marines had done the same things there. They had gone hand to hand in combat. Many had died. Jesus, save my ass and give me the strength!

When we dug holes that night, we kept exposing dead NVA. Eventually, I told the squad to scrape dirt around them and sit in for the night. Behind me was a stack of NVA packs. I was so tired that I couldn't find the energy to look at them.

The next morning, we were formed into security for the area and searched the entire ville for info and anything we could come up with.

I found a pouch with blooper rounds in it … Russian. It scared me to think these fuckers had some of the same weapons of destruction.

★★★

The next day McCarville and Second Platoon machine gunner Harmon became scavengers, finding NVA packs with North Vietnamese money, radios, weapons, a flag, maps, and supplies, including sandals, cigarettes, and khakis. They found a stack of NVA rifles in a fighting trench along one side of a rice paddy, all spread out and just waiting for their owners (no longer around) to jump into position for the ambush.

Many years later, in quieter and gentler times, I discovered that he had written about the pain of those days, confessing that he had left a small part of his soul at a stream that was dyed red with blood at Go Noi Island.

Over the next few days, we coordinated our sweeps with Mike and Lima Companies. On one such coordination, Mac told about meeting up with Mike Company after a squad of theirs had been ambushed. Here was the action as he remembered it:

We moved out in the early morning to back Mike Company 3/5. They took the point. You could hear the shit start to fly as soon as they were out in the next ville, and you knew they were catching shit. At that time, I was becoming the most senior member of the platoon, not the most experienced but the most senior … all twenty-one years of me. (All you had to do was to live long enough).

When we caught up with Mike, our lieutenant told me to accompany the lieutenant from Mike Company to the scene of the recent ambush. As we advanced up the line, I made contact with their lieutenant.

I advised my squad to look sharp and spread the fuck out. I did not need an ambush to start my day. All were locked, loaded, and ready to kick ass.

The lieutenant from Mike Company was upset (fucked up, if you will). As we advanced toward the point of contact, we saw gear tossed about—syringes, corpsman bags, helmets, and various other gear. On the other side of a small hooch was the battlefield—large amounts of brass, spoons from frags, half-empty magazines, and shit you knew marines did not let go.

After I set the squad into a perimeter and consolidated our radio contact with Kilo 6 actual and Kilo 2 actual, I asked the Mike Company lieutenant, "What now?" You could see that life ended here, and a lot of shit took place before it did. The lieutenant was kind of "not there."

I looked at the tree line, and we advanced together, with two riflemen and my radioman. We reached a trench behind the tree line first. The two riflemen were placed to both sides of the trench, far enough away not to hear comments by the lieutenant. The radioman puked at the sight in the trench and was left to our rear at my orders. Flanks were moved out farther and my best man, Vaca, was put toward the front.

In the trench lay six to eight bodies of marines. It was the squad that was ambushed. They had been stripped of their gear and clothes and then killed. Some had wounds through their arms and hands as if to ward off the final death blows. These men had been executed by the NVA!

The lieutenant became incoherent. He started babbling and crying. No shame—that's just the way it was. He mouthed their names and said repeatedly that they were still alive. I turned away and let him go. As time went by, Mike Company consolidated and relieved us. I pulled my squad in from the flanks and point and we returned to Kilo.

★★★

Being in weapons platoon now and carrying the 60 mm mortar, I was usually in close proximity to the CP (command post). It certainly wasn't always so. I now enjoyed *not* being on point or in the fray with McCarville or anyone else charging tree lines, clearing battlefields, sitting in two-man ambushes, or spending nights out on listening post. I'd been there, done that. And like tabasco sauce, a little bit goes a long way. Back at the CP, we had found a nice grove of trees near a village with small clearings to set up, regroup, and wait for the next encounter. It didn't take long.

A firefight erupted as Second Platoon approached the next tree line over. I think we were near the Le Bac ville. The villages there were all interconnected by well-worn paths through the forest, so you never knew for sure where you were, but it really didn't matter. It was mostly the same everywhere.

In the bush, there were no roads, no autos, no tractors, no power lines, and no sewers. There was only thick jungle forests, streams, open rice paddies (mostly dry now), cornfields, and rice paddy dikes. This was as rural as it got; there was no modern civilization, and we were in the bush! We were a long, long way from home.

Villages here were populated with thatched-roof huts held up by bamboo poles. There was no television, no telephones, no refrigeration, no electricity, and no mail. If the hooches had walls, they were thatched ones extending down from the roof. Oftentimes there would be an entire wall missing, leaving the inside open to the elements. There were no doors or windows. I didn't see furniture in the hooches. These people were peasant farmers—old men, old women, and children. No young men. They certainly weren't well educated, well fed, or well clothed. Their possessions seemed to be what they were wearing, some chickens, a plot of land, and sometimes maybe a water buffalo. They lived on what they grew.

In this area, we received most of our attacks from the villages (villes) as we approached. The VC or the NVA had come in, assassinated or intimidated the village leaders, and taken over. Charlie had food, supplies, and weapons stashed there in the village, and they had reasonable accommodations, much better than a trapdoor hole or tunnel in the jungle floor out in the bush. In addition, they had a subservient population. In some cases, they made the village into a medical hospital or supply center.

The fight began as Second Platoon swept through the area. There was always an initial volley, the back and forth, and then the artillery and the jets, with their bombs and napalm. The rice paddy dikes were trampled. The rice paddies were cratered. Some villages were burned or leveled by ordinance. When that happened, we relocated the people who survived.

I wondered what these people thought and felt with war all around them from both sides. They were subjugated and brutalized by the VC and the NVA. They were often in the middle of the back-and- forth fighting. Their crops might be destroyed, their villages might be burned, their prize water buffalo might be slaughtered, and they might be relocated to who knows where.

This was all in an effort to impose on them a government of one persuasion or another, either Communist or Western Democracy. In my opinion, these people didn't really care one way or another which side won. This was supposed to be a "Vietnamization" campaign to win their hearts and minds, but I wondered how many hearts and minds we were winning over like this? I was saddened by the brutality of this war on the civilian population.

I walked alongside villagers as we "resettled" them to another place. I saw pain and sadness in their faces as we walked away from their possessions. Now they had nothing, and nobody knew where they were going. I felt that these were nice, peaceful people completely vulnerable to anybody with a gun. I wished I could help them. Not being able to communicate made this even harder. I did not believe that this war was helping them.

The firefight out in front escalated until there was a sustained volley of small arms fire in both directions. I heard a machine gun. It appeared that the NVA weren't going to give up this patch of land, at least not without another fight. Out there, two hundred yards away, one of our squads was being hammered.

I wasn't out there. I was fearful for them and knew I must help however I could. It was a feeling that everybody in the company shared when a squad came under attack; you did everything you could to help. You forgot about your own safety. You did whatever it took.

From a small open clearing surrounded by trees and corn plants near the CP, I raced to set up the 60 mm mortar for our support. Brown (the ammo humper) brought his mortar rounds. He started unpacking the mortar rounds from their casings as Wilson (squad leader) relayed coordinates. He determined elevation and number of increments to be used on the rounds. I fired off several rounds while Brown continued collecting extra rounds from the grunts, who were all more than happy to donate them to the cause.

I always felt sorry for the "0311" infantry grunts who were tasked with carrying extra mortar rounds, extra machine gun belts, or extra 3.5-inch super bazooka rocket launcher rounds for us … in addition to their own gear.

There were more adjustments from Wilson and more rounds fired. After a while, I had twenty or more empty casings in a pile around the baseplate, where we had all teamed up to mortar the heck out of that far tree line. We hoped it helped and did some good. We wouldn't know until they got back.

A 60 mm mortar could do some serious damage to anyone nearby when it hit. It was like a big, powerful grenade with a blast range of twenty to twenty-five meters, so it must be taken seriously. It has a max fly range of up to two miles. It isn't just an offensive weapon; it is also used defensively. Besides hoping to inflict pain and suffering on the enemy, another purpose for lobbing the rounds onto them was to keep the enemy occupied and down low, not firing, so that our troops could race back to safety from wherever they might have been pinned down, usually an open field or rice paddy.

A mortar round has tail fins on the rear end for stability through the air. It has an explosive in the back end for propulsion and from one to four increments, which are small C-4 packets that can be added to give it extra oomph for extra distance, if needed. The round is dropped down the smoothbore mortar tube, hits the firing pin, and rockets up into a high parabola, dropping in right on top of the enemy.

I have had guys come to the mortar pit, shake my hand, and tell me they were able to get back from an ambush while the gooks were kept down as I walked the rounds horizontally, allowing the guys to sneak out just behind the explosions.

I also had a fire team tell me once that when they encountered gooks across a small river one night, nearly a thousand meters out from our CP. They said that the rounds I sent out most of the night kept the bad guys pinned down and unable to escape. In the morning at first light, the bad guys were trying to flee the area in a sampan down the river, and I actually hit and sank it with one of my mortar rounds. That, of course, was simply pure luck but very, very satisfying. Get some!

After the frenzied actions of providing mortar support for Second Platoon two hundred yards away, we waited for the artillery, air strikes, and then resupply—or the next attack. While we waited, Lieutenant Smith (our commanding officer) decided to call in the F-4 Phantom jets from the Da Nang Air Base and eliminate the opposition in that far tree line. He needed more firepower to rescue McCarville and the Second Platoon.

The lieutenant and the rest of the CP had a little area carved out near the edge of the tree line where they had a good view of the rice paddy and opposing tree line. Nobody knew it at the time, but Lieutenant Fred Smith would later go on to become the founder and CEO of Federal Express (FedEx). Smith was the Kilo Company commanding officer (the skipper), but he had the ability to lead and inspire his men without commanding by demanding. He told you what he wanted and you wanted to do it. He was one of the officers that I respected. He was good! He knew what he was doing, and he looked out for his men. Not all of the officers I met were good, knew what they were doing, or looked out for their men.

It had been quiet for some time when I heard the jets arriving. As I remember, they came in pairs. There were two of them. Brown, Weiber, Wilson, and I stood up at the edge of our tree line to watch the imminent action, standing side by side and just a few inches apart.

The jets came in right to left, single file, one after the other, diving to near treetop level at the far tree line just a few hundred yards away before releasing their cargo of bombs. Brown and I stood transfixed at our front-row seat, watching this delightful sight. It was quite a treat to watch the bad guys take a shellacking after the ambushes and booby traps they had imposed on us.

"Get some," said Brown in a Southern accent. Larry Brown was a good ol' country boy from a small town in Kentucky who definitely knew how to shoot. He had enough country know-how in him that he probably could have survived Vietnam all on his own without any of us. He had been with us for a long time and had accompanied us on all of our many patrols. "Get some" is the regiment slang for "Kill some."

And just as awesome as the jets with their firepower of bombs was the display of green tracers being fired back up at them by the gooks on the receiving end of those bombs. I can't imagine the guts it takes to stand up and look into the face of an incoming F-4 Phantom jet that's coming straight at you, aiming to release five-hundred-pound bombs on your position while you're trying to shoot it down with a little AK-47 rifle. But that's what they did. You have to admit that they had brass balls and they did walk the walk.

We watched the first attack, one jet and then the other. They climbed out steeply and circled around for another run. Lining up for the next run, they made their approach. Barreling down the pipe with green tracers coming back up at them all the way, they dropped their loads. The explosions were booming loud and threw up lots of dirt, dust, and debris into tall brown columns of smoke and dirt.

Brown and I were standing there next to each other, along with the other two, like spectators at a football game, cheering the spectacle of power and destruction, when I heard a strange rapid spinning and whirling/twirling sound.

For the life of me, I swear it sounded like a giant June bug flying at night back home in Minnesota. It was getting louder quickly. I couldn't see anything, but it was coming toward us fast. Without time to think or react, I heard a loud *whack* right next to me. Brown was thrown backward, grasping his leg.

He winced, crying out, "Ow, shit, damn it!" He had been hit right smack-dab in the leg by a ragged piece of flying shrapnel from the exploding bombs. From the sound of the whack, I thought he should be dead, but miraculously, it didn't kill him. It did slice up his thigh into a nasty gash and cut, and it seemed to have busted his kneecap. He would be another one medevacked out that day. I wouldn't see him again. I would miss him, though. He was good for laughs and good times, a real good ol' boy!

The realization wasn't lost on me that had it been two feet higher, he probably would have been killed, as it would have hit him smack in the face. Or if it had been two feet higher and two feet over to the side, I wouldn't have survived the day. How lucky we were!

I realized once again that in the bush, anything bad could happen at any time, anywhere, and to anyone. There was no rhyme and no reason. It was simply the happenstance of combat. Even so, we in this little group had dodged the bullet so far, but I was beginning to think that dumb grunts shouldn't be out pushing our luck by standing up watching five-hundred-pound bombs explode from two hundred yards. That probably wasn't the smartest thing we could have been doing. I was thinking that maybe it was a little like standing up in a firefight. This was another narrow escape that I'd add to my list. Returning to our makeshift mortar pit near the CP, I wondered how many close calls I'd had. How many did I get?

After the jets, it grew quiet again. None of us believed that being quiet for a time meant the bad guys had left. It just wouldn't be that easy. They were still out there resting and waiting. Or maybe they had disappeared in order to regroup somewhere else. Or maybe this time we got 'em.

While things were settled down a bit, the lieutenant decided what to do. We needed a rest and a resupply. We needed to evacuate the dead and wounded. We rested in the shade and waited for our helicopters to arrive with our resupply. A perimeter was set up. It was time for a C rations refresher.

I was sitting under a nice tree in some shade, sipping the syrup from a can of pineapple chunks, when I saw Doc Sinor walking my way. He grinned at me, which was unusual for him. Doc was usually a serious no-nonsense type of guy, unusually mature and seemingly educated. He was scholarly like a professor but without glasses. Maybe it was because as a navy corpsman attached to a marine combat unit, he had seen more action and medical emergencies than the average ER doc back home. At the ripe old age of twenty-three, he looked older and wiser than he was. Doc was the perfect example of a Middle American from "flyover country" in the US, coming from a small town in Oklahoma and being honest, straightforward, and hardworking. But he was also a jokester.

Robert L. Sinor stood about five feet eight inches and weighed probably 140 pounds soaking wet. He had a heap of blond hair on top of his head and a Marine Corp haircut on the sidewalls. His blond moustache was unusual for a marine but allowed, probably because he was actually navy, not USMC.

He wasn't wearing a flak jacket or a soft cover hat but was carrying his hard hat helmet. He had no weapon and no backpack. His silver dog tags dangled around his neck down to the green sweaty T-shirt. Jungle utilities and jungle boots completed the image of someone out enjoying a leisurely nonchalant summer stroll, at least during this respite. I wondered why he would be grinning, so I asked him.

"I wanted to find out how hot it is," he said, grinning sheepishly again as if he had just played a huge joke on somebody and gotten away with it. "So I stood my thermometer in the sand like a flagpole."

"So how hot is it?"

"I don't know because the mercury inside it got to the top of the thermometer and then broke the glass off the end and poured itself out onto the sand."

"Well, I guess it's hot!"

I wondered to myself if this could be true. It was either true and it was really hot (I already *knew* that it was really hot) or it wasn't true and he was smiling because he thought he'd pulled one over on me. Either way, it's a story I intended to remember. Most people wouldn't believe it.

In the meantime, Second Platoon had been recovered, relieved, resupplied, and renewed. We set in for the night and we'd get to do it all over again tomorrow—unless tomorrow brought some new fun surprises.

In war, as it is in life, chance rules the encounters we experience: who lives or dies, who is maimed or not, and who is allowed to skate through an encounter without harm is simply determined randomly by chance. It's called "happenstance." It has nothing to do with staying awake in class, paying attention, or how fast you can duck and cover. It is either your time or it is not.

There is a saying about that: "It may not be your time, but you can make it your time by standing up in a firefight." (The meaning, of course, is not to do something stupid.)

We were in one of our sweeps, trudging along only as fast as point could go. I was assigned to Third Platoon today. The squad I was with was not even point for our platoon, and we were spread out as per usual. I was somewhere in the middle.

I was carrying my 60 mm mortar and Tim McGuire was up ahead of me a few guys carrying his M60 machine gun. Tim was a tall guy, muscular with brownish-reddish hair, dull now from several days of dirt, sweat, and no showers. In fact, I couldn't remember our last shower. Hair got pretty well matted down like straw after a few days of sweating and sleeping in the dirt. Tim was in weapons platoon also, but I didn't know him well. The few times I'd talked with him, he was warm and friendly, with a big smile. I think he was Irish, and I think I remember a slight Irish accent.

On the march, a machine gunner carries the weapon over his shoulder, holding it level, with his hand on the barrel. This made it good for humping a heavy weapon long distances. Unfortunately, it also made it easy to spot a high-value target like a machine gunner. Tim was spotted, targeted, and shot through the chest when they opened up on us.

When we were ambushed by a volley of incoming small arms fire, as this was, the immediate response was to hit the deck, drop to the ground, face the incoming fire, and then return fire. Usually, as in this case, the firefight was over in less than a minute. The adrenaline flowed, the heart raced and pounded, and after the firing ceased, your hands started to shake. The fear kicked in. I found it strange that the fear kicked in after the fighting stopped.

The sound of incoming small arms crackling around your ears is something you can never forget. It actually hurt the ears, as those rounds were causing mini sonic booms as they flew past your ears, moving faster than the speed of sound. The good news was that if you could hear them, you hadn't been hit.

After the initial firefight, the lieutenant called in the F4 Phantom jets. This time they dropped napalm. I felt some satisfaction at seeing the bright flames and black smoke where the ambush had originated. Unfortunately, whoever attacked us had probably fled the area the minute we stopped our return fire and was long gone by the time the jets arrived. Later we would call in the CH-46 Chinook helicopters to remove Tim and medevac out any other dead or wounded.

As we waited, I was sitting alongside Tim. He had been covered by his own poncho. Only his boots stuck out the end, toes up. There was no blood or gore, at least not now and at least not in sight. The round had gone in clean and gotten him in the heart. He lay quiet and still. I daydreamed while staring at his dirty jungle boots covered with dry mud and rice paddy shit.

I wasn't particularly sad or distraught, maybe a little melancholy. I had only been here six months, but I had grown accustomed to it. Death was a fact of life here. It could happen at any time, in any place, and to any one of us. We all took our chances. I'm sorry for Tim but thankful it wasn't me. I thought it was better to be killed outright, like Tim, than to be mangled by a Bouncing Betty or a mine and writhing in pain, seeing your legs or arms blown off and your guts spilling out onto the ground. So thankfully, he didn't suffer. It was over, literally, in a heartbeat.

I was musing that ten or fifteen minutes ago, he had been alive, hauling his share, taking his chances, and sweating along with the rest of us. Now he seemed to be resting peacefully under a nice protective poncho, out of the sun and no longer worried about the heat, carrying his heavy load, or feeling hungry. He was at peace.

For a while, I contemplated chance and happenstance once again. It could have been me. Tim was but two or three guys ahead of me. Shit happens, and it happens suddenly. We never know how or why it happens. It just does. It's always random. I was wondering about the chances for me to get all the way through my tour and back to home. I still had more than half my tour left—about two hundred days and a wake up—give or take a few. This land did not seem to want us to go home alive, mentally or physically. I'd call this another close call. I added it to the list.

But then I suddenly got mad. I got mad at Tim! (Sometimes over there, we got crazy thoughts without even trying.) Tim had found the key to peace and safety. He was going to shrug off his load and get out of this damn place. He was going to get out of the heat and away from the mosquitos. He was going home, and I was not. He was simply going to leave this place that was trying to kill us all! And I got really mad when I realized it. I stood up and kicked him in the boots. I yelled at him to get up. That didn't work. He ignored me. I walked away pissed-off.

Unfortunately, Tim's friends in the other units wouldn't even miss him for some time. They didn't know about this incident yet, and it wasn't unusual for someone not to be around for a while. One day, though, someone would say, "Hey, has anyone seen McGuire? He hasn't been around for a while." People got separated from the companies and their platoons all the time for R & R, or in-country R&R, or sometimes they rotated home. Sometimes they were shipped off to a school for something or other. But suddenly, they simply were not around anymore. There were never any big announcements or parties, and usually nobody knew you left. Sometimes people were wounded and medevacked out, and sometimes they were killed and went home in a body bag.

Bastien and his 60 mm mortar just after a fire support mission for McCarville and Second Platoon on Operation Allen Brook

Doc Robert Sinor on Operation Allen Brook just before he tried to tell me how hot it was

Larry Brown on Allen Brook (above)

Anthony Weiber, goofing off as usual (ha!)

The result of a five-hundred-pound bomb drop from an F4 Phantom that sent shrapnel flying into Brown's leg on Operation Allen Brook

The temporary CP home for Kilo 3/5 on Operation Allen Brook. That's Company Commander Lieutenant Fred Smith drinking coffee while strategizing artillery and air strikes.

Farmers and their thatched roof homes…

The villes were populated by old men, old women, and children—no young men. Even though these men were old, they were still capable of firing rifles and setting booby traps. The guy above, second from the left, in the blue shirt, was killed trying to sneak through our perimeter one night when the VC launched an attack.

CHAPTER 3

FACING THE DRAGON

A Starlight Scope was state-of-the-art technology in night vision in 1968. The idea was to mount it on an M14 rifle and give it to a sniper. It was a four-power magnifier telescope that used ambient light (starlight) to intensify and display images through a green cathode-ray tube to the eyepiece. Tower personnel and marines also used it out on listening posts to watch for enemy movement at night. I had the opportunity one night to look through one and could see clearly a squad movement approaching us at about a hundred yards, contrasted against a completely black jungle background. It was impossible to see them with unaided eyesight. A Starlight Scope was an awesome advantage. It would mean death to many marines if it ever got into the wrong hands.

We continued to play hide-and-seek with Charlie, looking to engage and then destroy him. That's why we were there. And the enemy returned the favor with equal intensity back at us, except they usually determined the time and the location of the contact. It was a nightmarish situation for all concerned. Nobody liked it. Yet there we were.

Sometimes shit happens and you are the one standing in it. It's happenstance. How we react to that shit is what is important. It determines if you get to go home. If you do go home, it determines what you will think about, at least subconsciously or in your dreams, for the rest of your life. It never leaves you entirely. It resides within, sometimes festering deep down, sometimes just below the surface. And if or when it ever does surface again, it will be triggered by some random event bringing back the memories all of a sudden, like a freight train barreling out of a tunnel. So we did what we needed to do, what was needed at the time, in order to survive. There really was no other choice.

The following is an account of the actions and what it was like, by Ron McCarville, in his own words, simply doing what had to be done at the time to get through a few days and one day in particular. That day was just another day at the office, but this one earned him the Bronze Star.

> On May 20, 1968 (my birthday), we assaulted a bunker line that had steel reinforced tops on them. The steel was rails from the railroad that crossed Go Noi Island. I really thought I would die that day. I always saw a tombstone in my mind with "born on" and "died on" being the same date. It haunted me.
>
> I knew that if I could get through this day, I would survive. Screaming and running, shooting for all I was worth, we reached the trench alongside the bunkers. They were empty. Damn, I was relieved. Our commanding officer, Lieutenant Smith, had "artied" the hell out of things before we went in—and God bless him for it.
>
> On or around May 24 (or maybe May 23) was when Corporal Perkins stepped on a mine. We were still saddling up. We had palace guard that day, and he hit the mine. The lieutenant called for us to get to him ASAP, and we did. As I approached with my squad, I saw Perkins down on the side of the railroad tracks and thought, You dumb shit, why

did you walk on a trail? I could see he was hit in the face and the head, and his foot was screwed up.

I snapped. I set the squad out, got a radioman by me (Herbert Lash, Pennsylvania), and cried like a baby. I wanted out—any way I could get out. I wanted out. Perkins and I would have rotated home at the same time. No one from 3/5 had rotated in for a while without getting hit bad or KIA. I knew I was next.

On May 27, 1968, I faced my dragon. I don't know that I won, but they didn't kill me physically. Part of my soul must still be there. Every man who has ever been in Vietnam has faced the dragon. Some of us were lucky enough to walk out.

I have thought long and hard about the story I am about to relate to you. It is not easy, and it burns in my soul. I wish there were a more detailed way to relate the facts as I recall them—locations, names, and so forth. But I am using my memory, which is not what it used to be, so excuse me for mistakes. They are unintentional.

On the early morning of May 27, 1968, nothing seemed different except the fact that 3/5 was going to retrace their steps of the previous day. Any warrior knows that is a mistake. Hell, it was taught to you in training. "Never use the same trail twice; always avoid paths if possible."

The preceding day, someone had lost a Starlight Scope, and it hadn't been recovered. It lay in our path from the previous day, and now we were going to reverse course and search for it. There would be hell to pay if it was not recovered, so the task was at hand. The die was cast.

Lima took point, with Kilo following. My squad was point for Kilo, and we crossed a dry riverbed to a ville and tried to hook up with Lima. They had advanced quickly and were far into the ville by the time my point man caught up to them. They were taking incoming mortars, small arms, and machine gun fire.

I informed Kilo 2 *actual* that I had contacted Lima and was hooking up on-line with them. He apparently had his own problems, pinned down by automatic weapons fire, and ordered me, "Hold your position until the rest of the company and battalion are across the riverbed and into the ville."

Upon getting the squad down and under cover, I approached a "tail-end Charlie" for Lima and asked what was going on. They were about what looked like a squad or two down, and no one was talking. I yelled at the man and asked again, "What the fuck is going on, man?" No reply.

A few heads jerked up and looked back at me, but no one spoke. I guess it was a stupid question with mortar rounds landing all about and rounds cracking over your head. I got back on the radio and informed Kilo 2 actual that shit was happening and he needed to get up here. He told me again to hold my position.

Shortly after this radio conversation, Lima moved out toward the firing, the point of contact into the ville. No word was passed, nor was there radio contact with Lima. They just jumped up and ran forward.

I informed the lieutenant again of the situation, and he ordered me forward. "Keep in contact with Lima. We are on the way." We caught up to the tail end of Lima again. They were now on-line, and shit was starting to fly—lots of incoming fire.

To our direct front was the sound of a crew-served weapon. It sounded like a heavy machine gun. The squad was secure in the tree line, and gun team leader Harmon and I exchanged weapons with the gun crew. I took the .45 and several mags, along with several frags. It was my belief that the NVA did not know where we were, and I thought we could get to them and eliminate the gun.

We were about twenty to twenty-five meters from the squad, and I heard gooks talking. We were in the low crawl and getting ready to do the shit. At this point, my radioman stood up and yelled, "Mac, the lieutenant wants to talk to you."

I knew we were in deep shit now. We both threw frags and hauled ass back to the squad. Rounds were buzzing around like hornets. The gun team started working out, and the squad was laying down a base of fire. I informed the lieutenant of our current situation, and he ordered me to hold my position. He was sending up a sniper team to deploy as I saw fit.

Our position was now known to the NVA, and they were pouring it on us. The snipers arrived and were standing up looking around. I directly ordered them to get down. Just about this time, both were hit and fell on me. I was cussing them and bandaging them at the same time. Jesus Christ!

By now, things were getting untenable. Lima moved about 150 to 200 meters to our rear. No contact with them or any word about their maneuver was passed to us.

I ran to Lima's position and dragged a corpsman with me to the snipers, helping them return to the Lima position. I returned to my squad. By this time, shit was falling apart. I sent the gun team back with the fire team to join the remaining members of my squad.

I now realized I was alone. Rounds were falling around me like rain. I raised my M16, and it was shot out of my hands. I picked up a sniper's bolt-action weapon and jacked rounds through it until they were gone.

Another M16 was there, so I emptied it and was now without a loaded weapon. I jacked another mag into the M16 and picked up the weapons scattered by snipers and the gun team in the confusion. I was hauling five weapons, and shit was raining down on me.

I couldn't understand why I was not getting hit. Mortar rounds were landing around me, and it was like slow motion. The ground was exploding around me, but nothing happened to me. I then hauled ass to the trench that Lima and my squad were in. My lieutenant was on the radio, and I inform him that shit was deep and I needed reinforcement now. He ordered me to hold my position.

Lima was to my left; my squad was to my right. They were all down, and no one was shooting. I started screaming at people to get up and shoot. Some had passed out from the heat, and some were wounded.

I got bewildered looks from people as I walked up and down the top of the trench yelling. I must have appeared to be a crazy son of a bitch. Incoming increased, and there was movement to our front. The gun team was down. The squad was down. And Lima was down.

With the assistance of Corporal Vaca, we pulled all the men behind the trench into a tree line for cover. Vaca passed out, and I dragged him back. The radioman was babbling and passed out. I gave him my last canteen over his head and dragged him back.

I searched the trench for a workable weapon. All were jammed. The gun had half a belt left, and the barrel was smoking. I fired it off, and that was it. I got on the radio and informed the lieutenant that I need*ed* arty now. The ammo was low, and the people were down. I was the only one standing.

As arty rounds started coming in, I adjusted the fire toward us. The NVA were in front of us, and I could see bushes moving. There was no breeze, so I knew they were moving in. One or two rounds landed around the trench, and all you could see were flying bodies.

I started throwing frags because that was all I had. I could see parts of bodies flying up in front of me. The air strikes started, and I could hear the NVA firing at the jets as they reached the bottom of their run, their lowest point to the ground. I threw frags in that direction, and slowly the fire receded.

At one point, I fixed a bayonet to an M16 and thought I would not make it out of the trench. No one was moving. Everyone was down, and I could see movement in front of me. No ammo, just frags. I thought I was going to die. Truly!

You reach a point where there is complete peace. I know that sounds weird, but it seemed that way. The finality of knowing or thinking you are certainly going to die takes on a determination that you will do what you have to do. It is a foregone conclusion and you are along for the ride.

This ordeal lasted nine hours. It seemed forever to me. Toward the end of the day, I became aware that I could not hear. Many rounds had cracked over my head, and coupled with arty and air strikes, it had temporarily taken my hearing.

Reinforcements finally arrived with Sergeant Austin and some ammo. The FNGs cleared and loaded M16s while I emptied magazine after magazine. As weapons jammed, I grabbed another and kept up the firing. The FNGs (fucking new guys) were crying, and I tried to calm them, but I didn't know if I did.

I never saw them again after the next morning and didn't even know who they were, except that they were marines.

At one point, I can remember a man from Lima looking at me from the trench. I looked over at him briefly and kept firing. He stood up and started firing his weapon. That was the catalyst. Then they all started firing. Things simmered down after a while, and I was dazed. I was scared and shaking.

Some canteen found its way to me, and I drained it. I recalled not having water since early that morning and was dizzy.

My lieutenant, along with the Kilo Company commanding office and Lima Company commanding officer, came to my position. They asked in detail what had happened. I told them as best I could. It was, as I recall, when Lima moved back approximately 150 to 200 meters that I heard screams from their most forward position and was certain I heard calls for help. I may have been mistaken. I hoped I was.

I do believe that any air strikes or artillery I called in may have killed anyone to our front. I pray that there were no marines left out there. It has been a heavy burden to live with for a long time. I was later to find out that we faced a platoon of NVA, or so I was informed by a citation. All I know is there seemed to be no lack of lead flying at my ass that day. I know I killed some NVA. I could not honestly tell you how many.

Mistake nothing about this recollection; it is mine alone. I hope that one day it sheds some light on one instance of one very small battle in Vietnam.

★★★

As mentioned, that recollection was McCarville's. The citation refers to the Bronze Star. My recollection of that day is pumping out mortar rounds to help and watching jets come in dropping their five-hundred-pound bombs. Only two hundred yards separated us that day, but we were miles apart. We were so close and yet so far apart. None of us knew, or could know, what McCarville and the Second Platoon were going through. I was never really threatened that day; they were threatened all day long. Two hundred yards and yet worlds apart …

CHAPTER 4

ON OPERATION

It was now sometime in June 1968. It was after the Robert F. Kennedy assassination in early June. We had been on Allen Brooke for a couple of weeks by then. I lost track of time and the days when they all ran together, with no end in sight. I tried to keep track of things by noting the significant events and when they happened, such as the Martin Luther King assassination in early April or the Tet Offensive that began on January 31 or February 1.

We had no goals other than to meet the enemy, kill him, or move him out of the area, hoping to get through the day alive ourselves in the process. We swept, searched, and destroyed. Some of our guys had come to grief early on, but the firefights, ambushes, and booby traps were fewer now. Things had settled down into a quiet recurring daily grind. Some days were a little interesting; most were not. The daily grind was long, hot, and boring, tiring and monotonous, day after day.

Either we had killed them all or they had run off to regroup and have another go at us later. I didn't believe for a minute that we had killed them all. They would be back, just not now.

Our routine had become consistent and that was worrisome. On the one hand, it was comforting to be doing the same thing every day, especially if we did not find and engage the enemy. That meant a day without injury or death and one less day left in the Nam. We just wanted to survive long enough to go home. Nobody really cared about body counts for HQ.

On the other hand, it was a bit unnerving. There was some rule of thumb against doing the same thing twice or becoming too consistent, too complacent. Sweeping and searching during the day, we looked to make contact but hadn't found any recently. Nobody was unhappy about that. Our attitude came off as more along the lines of a favorite jarhead saying: "We are the unwilling, led by the unqualified, to do the unnecessary." From our cynical point of view, that pretty much summed it up. But in reality, it was simply a standard marine bitch, one among many others.

Stopping at twilight, we hunkered down as best we could, wherever we were. It seemed too predictable to me, and I imagined Charlie was watching our every move. I felt like we were a slow-moving massive elephant being hunted by the fast, agile, stealthy lionesses. We had the firepower, but they had the stealth and the jungle skills. They had lived in this land for centuries. The only reason we were winning here, if you can call it that, was the brute force of artillery, air power, and massive deployment of troops and weapons. I thought it must have been an enormous cost to run this war … I couldn't even imagine and had no clue.

At night, ambush squads were dispatched, and two-man listening posts were stationed outside the perimeter. The rest of us manned our places on the perimeter, each location with two or three marines rotating watch throughout a long dark night at two-hour intervals.

Three-hour intervals gave the marine on watch too much time to doze off. Our exhaustion was explained by twelve-hour days in the hot sun, clearing an area, hauling heavy loads, and crossing rivers and streams to inspect villages for enemy weapons or food. Then we'd do two or three two-hour watches at night. And these were the good days, with no enemy contact.

Every marine on watch fought a body and a mind that simply wanted to doze off into a deep sleep. Sleep beckoned my mind and body with remembrances of a warm blanket on a soft couch during a cold Minnesota winter's night. It was a fight of willpower to keep eyes open and mind alert, a fight that so easily could be lost, even on a wet, muddy, moldy insect-ridden jungle floor in the rain.

It was so dark, so quiet, and so still that I could hear a snake slithering through the ground vegetation or a cricket chirping. I could hear a mosquito buzzing at a hundred yards. Most nights it was pure blackness. The blackness drove the other senses to work overtime, so I was hearing twigs snap, leaves rustle, and little animals scamper, all leading the mind to imagine Charlie sneaking up on me.

The imagination pushed fear into overdrive. On a dark night on watch, I would be anxious, heart racing and adrenaline pumping. I listened so hard that I thought my ears would break. I found that staying awake and alert on watch was the hardest reality about being in Vietnam. Generally, it was quiet, dark, warm, and boring. Sometimes it was dark, cold, and wet. It was always terrifying.

For two hours on watch, there was generally nothing to do but dwell on home, parties long past, high school friends, or school not yet finished. I reflected back on high school acquaintances, some liked and some not liked. I decided that even the ones I didn't particularly care for back then were probably not all that bad and that I would like the opportunity to be friends with them once again. I hoped I got that chance. My arrogant attitudes from those days had been beaten back by the loneliness here and the loss of their friendship. I had begun to understand now how the loss of something, once taken for granted, becomes very precious after it's lost. I'll surely do things differently next time, if I get that chance.

For my two hours, I'd think of almost everything that had ever happened in my past. I'd roll through my history and almost every encounter that had ever occurred. I was able to get through the two-hour shift without drifting off. But now what did I have left to think about during my next two-hour shift in the darkness? Or what would I think about in the one after that?

I decided that next time I'd just do it all over again but I'd change the outcomes somewhat. I'd imagine them different and better! This game kept me awake through several shifts. It was repetitive and boring, but it seemed to work. It worked so well in fact that I was no longer sure what the real truth of my life was anymore. I'd messed up my own personal history. I no longer remembered my own story and what really happened back then. I'd gotten it all screwed up. Oh well, what the heck, how important could that be, anyway? I'd remember it correctly someday.

On one of my watches, I wandered off topic. I began to think about this war. I thought about the deaths on both sides, the mutilation injuries that destroyed lives, and the cynicisms being grown in everyone about the government and our reasons for being here. Every one of us had our own reasons for being here, but there was questioning by some about the big picture. I was no different than anyone else. I saw the carnage to Americans and to the Vietnamese people and their country. I wondered, *Is this really necessary? What are we doing here?* I reminded myself that I planned to think more about this later, when I was home, after it was over.

It has been said of pilots that their jobs consist of hours and hours of boredom and every once in a while a few minutes of extreme fear. Our jobs there were much the same. The consistency and repetitiveness of our routine was comforting. But it was not safe or smart to be so predictable. I was apprehensive. Like driving on the freeway, I felt safe but wary of the cars near me. Complacency kills. Falling asleep on watch kills marines. Would those other guys stay awake? I could stay awake … but could they? We had heard many stories of squads being wiped out because the guy on watch fell asleep. It was just so hard to stay awake and alert. The people back home didn't know, didn't have a clue.

It was on one of those very nights that I came to revere, respect, and love the full moon. On first watch, there was no moon. The night and surroundings were as dark as in a cave. Encircled by trees and bushes looking into a pitch-black forest, I had only sound to alert me to somebody or something sneaking in on me. It was a terrifying time throughout the entire two-hour watch. I strained, hardly breathing, to hear anything out of the ordinary.

On second watch, a full yellow-gold moon came up over the trees across the rice paddy. A soft, friendly glow, it bathed everything in a light milky whiteness. I could have read a newspaper by the light. There was not going to be anybody sneaking in on me that watch. I could see through the trees and the bushes out onto the paddy. *That* was when I decided that I would forever onward salute the full moon whenever I saw it. I have been true to that vow ever since, although usually silently and secretly. To this day, there is no better sight than a full moon illuminating my backyard and the vegetation in the common area on the hill behind it.

On one of our moonless nights, I was in the bush on watch and Charlie was probing the lines. When we found and engaged Charlie or when we were attacked, we would often call for illumination rounds. They were sent our way by 81 mm mortars or, more usually, by 155 mm artillery canons miles away. At night, an illumination round was our best friend. While it lasted, it was as bright as a full moon. These ninety-two-pound shells carried a canister of lifesaving light that deployed a magnesium flare that descended under a parachute. It was a simple idea that worked well.

The tricky part was that somehow the artillery battery had to figure out how to send that round out to our exact location so that it arrived at exactly the right altitude and time (usually about six hundred meters above us) to expel the parachute and flare, which would burn for two minutes as it slowly descended. It was timed to just burn out as it hit the ground. That part was amazing. The deployment was actually a beautiful thing.

When the shell deployed the flare, it made a soft *pop* sound as the flare was expelled. It was usually made against a deadly silent backdrop where everyone around was holding their breath, listening for the bad guys moving in toward us. The pop echoed softly against silent forest walls. Usually there were no other sounds in the entire area and you would normally be able to hear a pin drop. It was an eerie silence accentuated by the anticipation of the coming light.

That *pop* was the most reassuring sound I could remember, as it signaled that we would soon be bathed in one million candlepower for two minutes. This was enough light to light up a one-thousand-square-meter grid and the entire area around us. We had two minutes to spot trouble. Charlie wouldn't be moving in during these two minutes. As it descended, you could hear the flare burn. It gave off a soft, sputtering hiss, much like a Fourth of July fireworks sparkler, which encased the entire area in an unreal and eerie magical feeling. The flare spun and twisted slowly as it descended, sending creepy, scary shadows scampering across the landscape.

When we were engaged with the VC or NVA, the artillery battery could send up several rounds over a wider area or they could send up several, one after the other, so that the night sky stayed lit up until the need was over. Illumination rounds deprived the enemy of their ability to sneak and surprise.

Another awesome device that we used occasionally was a trip wire and flare. Sometimes we set a trip wire that was attached to one or more flares. It was used to warn against incoming bad guys. When the trip wire was disturbed, the flare was activated, the fuse popped, and it started the flare burning for a minute to a minute and a half. It was a very bright light in a small area.

Sometimes a squad out on ambush would set a trip wire and flare, along with a Claymore mine. When the enemy tripped the wire and the flare went off, the person on watch fired the remote-controlled

Claymore. A Claymore was a concave-shaped mine sitting above ground and facing outward toward the enemy. It had an effective range of fifty to fifty-five yards and shot out small metal pellets similar to BBs, acting much like a shotgun blast. It was fired by a remote manual trigger.

On one particular night ambush, a squad from Third Platoon, probably Third Squad, had deployed several hundred meters out from the CP, down along one of the trails. Finding a nice thick bunch of vegetation for cover, they set up along the trail and placed a trip wire flare and Claymore at the far end of their ambush. Five slept, while one was always on watch.

Sometime during the night, the trip wire flare was triggered. Everyone woke up and was immediately consumed with fear. You could smell the stench of fear. That would normally have been the time for the guy on watch to activate that Claymore mine. However, whoever it was on watch at that time had some premonition against setting off the Claymore. He didn't "feel" right about it. He didn't blast the mine. The squad, however, blasted the area with their M16s and then sat up awake the rest of the night. It was a night of terror on the trail.

In the morning, at first light, after a quiet remainder of the night, when they got up to come back into the company CP, they checked the Claymore at that end of their ambush. They saw that it had been turned around facing them! Had they blasted it, they would have blown themselves away.

There is nothing scarier, that will get your attention faster, than a trip flare going off at night twenty-five to fifty feet away while you are on a dark jungle trail with no moon and no illumination rounds. Someone or something, whether it was human or animal, tripped that flare.

In this case, the NVA or VC knew very well that there was a squad lying in ambush there and that they had set a trip wire with a flare and a Claymore mine. The game being played that night was that one lone VC or NVA crawled up to the Claymore, turned it around, and then backed off before intentionally tripping the wire while leaving the scene of the crime. Charlie knew jungle warfare, and he owned it. We were only novice participants in this game.

I remember telling whoever was relating this story to me, "You must have been so scared that you sneezed in your snuggies."

He said, "Huh? What does that mean?"

I replied, "It's just a nice way to say shit your pants."

★★★

Settling in for the night (any night), for the rest of us not on ambush or listening post, meant we formed two-man teams in order to link our two ponchos together and build a two-man tent. These poncho tents look like pup tents, with a stick at each end holding up the two ponchos and linking them together through large grommet holes. The ponchos were flayed out and staked into the ground by shorter sticks or even rocks. In some cases, we even linked four together to make hotel-sized hooches.

Poncho tents were open at both ends. Rain and wind entered at will, but the ponchos did keep most of the rain out unless it was windy. When stopping on a slope or in a gully, it allowed any rain to wash right on through. There were no floors in these poncho tents. The ground, grass, weeds, mud, clay, or tree roots comprised the floor. I'd awakened many times to a small river flowing through my poncho tent, soaking my poncho liner blanket and me. If it rained, we'd get wet one way or the other. You got used to it. You never liked it. But that was life in the bush.

A funny thing about the monsoons in Vietnam, which usually last May through November, was that it was so brutally hot and humid during the day that you prayed for rain. But as soon as the sun was about to set and cool off, the clouds built up and it rained a heavy but usually short downpour. It was a cold rain, the rain you prayed for a few hours ago. But if you got wet now, you'd be wet, cold, and shivering all night. If you got caught in the rain, you'd get drenched in the rain. If the wind blew, you would be cold.

It wasn't the actual number on the thermometer. It was the drop in temperature. I could get accustomed to a daytime temperature of 110, but a drop of 30 to 40 degrees down to 70 or 80, or even just 90, was a big drop. Once given the word that we were stopping here, it was a race to build those two-man poncho tents before it rained. Sometimes we made it; sometimes we didn't. Pity the poor guy who didn't make it.

Gerald Baltes was a good friend from our Twins Platoon boot camp days at MCRD in San Diego. He was with us in weapons platoon. On one of those nights, I got my poncho tent made just in time. He did not make it in time. He was drenched. It was worth getting wet (for me) to run out into the rain for a quick moment and snap his picture. I laughed at the sad, forlorn look on his face as I snapped it with my Instamatic. I'd keep this one forever. Ha! Several years later, I attend his wedding in St. Paul, Minnesota, and I reminded him of this night when he was such a sad sack. Baltes was another warrior who was later seriously wounded but survived with a sense of humor.

Raining at sunset happened often, but this night was clear. It was still June and in the middle of the monsoons, but it would be dry tonight! A perimeter had been set; the night patrols and listening posts had been dispatched. Wilson and I were here with the Third Platoon, somewhere near the CP, and we had our watch requirements set. Wilson and I would take turns alternating two-hour shifts in the makeshift mortar pit and two-hour shifts sleeping in the "tent."

Watch would start later, when it was dark. Now we had time to sit and eat some "delicious" C rations chow in the fading light. I was having my favorite, spaghetti in the big can. I wrangled the can open with my trusty P-38 "John Wayne" can opener, leaving the lid attached to be used as a pot handle. With a few rocks, I created a nice three-pointed tripod table to rest my spaghetti can on, and I gently placed the heat tab under that. Half a heat tab allowed the spaghetti to heat up nicely in the can. Use an entire heat tab, however, and the extra heat expanded the spaghetti up and out of the can until it lost its balance and fell onto the ground in a big red messy splat. Ask me how I know.

Wilson was eating ham and lima beans, another favorite. Ha! It was so much a favorite that most marines referred to them as "ham and MFers." Some C ration meals were actually good; some not so much.

C rations came packaged in cardboard boxes containing food in cans and an accessory pack. They contained everything necessary for a "tasty" self-contained take-out meal or for eating on the run. The main course meals included meatballs and beans, beans and franks, chopped ham and eggs, beefsteak with potatoes and gravy, beef slices, sliced ham, boned chicken, boneless turkey, and chicken noodle soup. It was a good array of items, but it still became repetitive over a year.

Most of these came soaked in some form of glutamate preservative that disappeared when heated and seemed to be almost a tasty, fatty addition. But when you were forced to eat it cold, it was a clump of whitish-gray goo, not nice to look at or to eat. There was usually another can included, which might be a can of apricots, pears, fruit cocktail, pineapple, or peaches. And we usually had a dessert that was a cookie, a candy, a nut roll, a pound cake, or a fruitcake. Overall, it wasn't too bad.

The included accessory pack had everything you'd need for life in the bush: a plastic spoon for eating the meals, a P-38 "John Wayne" can opener so that you could get to the food, chewing gum, cigarettes (Chesterfields, Camels, or Marlboros), matches, salt and pepper, a heat tab for cooking the meal, dehydrated coffee or chocolate, creamer substitute, and that especially all-important toilet paper. It was not a happy experience to be without toilet paper in the bush.

I'd estimate that probably 90 percent of all our meals in Vietnam were C Ration meals eaten in the bush. Maybe 10 percent of our meals were from a mess hall, with hot "real" food.

Being out on operation for days or weeks at a time became monotonous, and we were vulnerable to many mundane health issues. I found that some of the more common problems with life in the bush on operation were that we didn't shower, didn't change clothes, and didn't take our boots or socks off. There weren't enough real medicines for normal problems. We didn't have access to lotions, salves, or creams. There was a lot of heat rash that might or might not get better in the average grunt. I never experienced that, but marines were out under the sun all day. The skin dried and burned. Insects and microbes burrowed in. That took a toll on the skin and scalp.

Most grunts seldom took off their boots and socks. Feet got wet in the rice paddies, streams, and rivers every day. This led to immersion foot (foot rot)—or so I hoped, in order to return home. Unfortunately for me that also never occurred, but my feet did get pale white and there was a lot of flesh that I peeled away when I did get to remove boots and socks.

Jungle rot was simply an outcome of living in high temperatures, high humidity, and high stress. Clothes rotted. Boots fell apart. Resupply helicopters usually brought a limited supply of clothes and boots, along with ammunition, food, and water. I personally received three or four pairs of new utilities and T-shirts over the course of my tour. I still have my fourth pair of jungle boots, which show the scars of our last combat missions. I look at the creases and scars across the top of them, caused by exploding shrapnel, and I still wonder how it managed to miss me.

Oftentimes we got our water out of wells located by the rice paddies. Of course, it was untreated, and if we didn't add our halazone tablets, as suggested, we were open to dysentery. This was our personal decision, but I often took the chance simply because I was thirsty and didn't want to wait. Our scout, Brown, was of the same opinion, and I followed his example. I have a great picture of him refilling canteens from a well next to a rice paddy.

Okay, truth be told, I did get the runs (diarrhea) a few times, not dysentery as I hoped, which probably would have warranted a medical evacuation. I discovered that the simple solution for diarrhea was to trade my pound cake, cigarettes, or whatever I could for all the peanut butter I could get. Peanut butter is a great "plugger-upper." Unfortunately, it takes two to three days to be effective, and that usually outlasted the toilet paper supplied with C rations. You can talk about terror in Vietnam, but running out of toilet paper while you have diarrhea was the absolute number one terror on my list. However, eventually peanut butter always works, and I use it still to this day.

Overall, not even including the bad guys, this land was filled with animals, insects, plants, heat and cold, bad water, disease, extremes, and a malevolent weather environment not friendly or welcoming to Americans. It wanted us out of here. And we truly would have liked to accommodate.

Life in the bush was full of strange ironies. For example, I don't remember being paid while I was in Vietnam, except for two times. The first time was while we were out on operation, in the bush far from anywhere. It was another hot afternoon, and we were stopped in a dry field. A perimeter had been set and manned around the field. I had no idea what was going on.

A CH-46 Chinook helicopter arrived, landed, and shut down. A couple of marines unloaded a long folding table and set it up a short distance from the helicopter. They added two folding chairs and covered the table with a long green cloth. A first lieutenant pay officer and a sergeant assistant, both dressed in brown khakis shirts, green trousers, and black spit-polished leather shoes, sat down at the table and opened a large three-ring ledger binder. They had a big box of money. They looked as if they were directly from accounting in headquarters out of Washington, DC, or something. The money they brought wasn't real US money. It was MPC (military payment currency) but it is was as good as US money in Vietnam. It was the only money accepted in addition to Vietnamese currency. It had different colors for different denominations.

They called us to the table one by one alphabetically. They asked us each how much of our monthly pay we wanted to keep on account with them and how much cash we wanted? I thought I was making about $115 per month but had nowhere to spend it except with the kids who sold us Cokes that they had stolen from the army; I took $15 for Cokes and left $100 on the books.

Mobeck had the same rank as me, but when it was his turn, he took $30 cash and left $220 on the books. He got paid $250! Later, when he told us that, we asked, "What the hell were you thinking? You don't earn that kind of money."

Mobeck laughed and said, "If they want to give me that much, I'll take it."

"They're gonna find out about the mistake, and they'll come get it and put you in the brig."

Mobeck just laughed.

The second time I remember was also out on operation, maybe four or five months later. It was the same thing. I was still getting my $115 per month. Mobeck was still getting around $250 per month. He took another $30 in cash and left another $220 on the account.

I don't know why we weren't paid while in the rear. At least, I don't remember being paid back at base. Maybe it was because we were hardly ever there. I'm sure they credited my account monthly, even if I didn't have a chance to pick it up. I do remember that when I went on R & R sometime in July, I did withdraw about $1,000. I don't know if Mobeck was ever found out.

Another interesting aspect of being on operation in the bush was "mail call." Sometimes on the resupply choppers, they brought out our mail. Mail was our only connection to family, friends, and the real world. I never saw a telephone while I was in Vietnam. There were no telephones, no cell phones, no texting, no email, and no connection to the world … at least for us out in the bush. We were literally worlds apart. So it was a big deal when we did have a mail call.

It was usually a happy time, but all the guys feared getting a "Dear John" letter from a wife or girlfriend. That was always a possibility and was anticipated more and more the longer the time since receiving the previous letter. One day when we got a mail call delivery, everyone was sitting around reading their good news. Then we heard it, a sad, muffled voice saying, "Oh no … I can't believe it."

Everybody knew that somebody had just received his Dear John letter. There were understanding smiles and chuckling all around. It's okay—join the club.

During some of the quiet times when we'd just sit around, which were quite frequent, long, and boring, I would write home to family or friends. I had a pen but no paper, no envelopes, and no stamps. No problem … I'd take an empty C rations cardboard box and rip off the ends so that I had only the bottom part, which was mostly blank cardboard about the size of a large postcard.

I wrote my short letter or note on one side, and then I wrote the "to" address and my "from" address on the other side. Then I wrote "free" where the stamp would normally be placed.

These "letters" were collected by the company gopher and were mailed out from the battalion headquarters base. It worked. We had *free* mail service. I sent a few off to Mom and Dad and friends. They all got a big kick out of those C ration postcards. I even sent one to Robert F. Kennedy when he was running for president, but I never got a reply because he was assassinated shortly after I sent it. But at least there was one advantage to being in Nam: free postage on C rations boxes made into postcards!

There was often so much quiet time, boring time, nothing-to-do time that we often just sat and shot the shit, talking about nothing. We talked about anything, everything, and nothing simply to fill the void. One night before dark, Wilson and I were having one of those discussions over our C ration meals, talking to fill the emptiness.

In between bites of my spaghetti, I asked Wilson how he came to be in the Nam. Wilson was a skinny young Southern gentleman. He came from Georgia and had a pleasant Southern accent. He was always polite and always mild-mannered. I don't remember him ever swearing, which was very unusual for a Marine Corps grunt. His tone was always upbeat and his talk always optimistic. He was a Christian. He was a good friend, and I was happy that he was around.

Lyndon Wilson stood about five feet ten inches and weighed between 120 and 130 pounds. We could be clones, except that he was skinny as a rail and didn't wear glasses. You could see his ribs when he breathed. He talked about how he always wanted to be an aviation mechanic. His recruiter had told him that in exchange for a four-year commitment, he would be sent to aviation mechanic school and that would be his MOS (military operations specialty). That's what he wanted, so he signed on the dotted line.

"So why are you *here* in the bush with us grunts in weapons platoon?" I asked.

"Oh that. I failed a written test and then got into an argument with the instructor about it."

"So they booted you out because of one silly test and argument?"

"Well, no, it happened more than once."

Wilson didn't seem particularly disappointed or cheated by the transfer to infantry status. But he then had well over two years left, plenty of time to do this tour and then get sent back again. I only had the rest of this tour and a few months more remaining in the Marine Corps before I was out. I didn't go any further into the details of his transfer. He just said that he'd finish mechanic school later, when he got out. And he did. He became an excellent aircraft mechanic and esteemed restorer of vintage aircraft.

After a lengthy silent pause, Wilson asked me, "So how did you manage to get here? Who did you piss off?"

Vincent and Mobeck in their two-man poncho tent

Bastien standing next to a four-man poncho tent, waiting for the next patrol

Gerald Baltes getting his poncho tent set up just *after* the daily monsoon shower. He would be wet, cold, and shivering most of the night.

I delightedly took this picture because my poncho tent was made just in time.

Our scout, Brown, collected well water because we had not been resupplied with fresh water for some time. When you're thirsty, it tastes just as good as fresh.

CHAPTER 5

BEGINNINGS

Getting to Vietnam actually wasn't hard at all. Some would say that it was a smart move, getting a two-year enlistment rather than the standard three or four. I said I beat the draft by enlisting in the USMC. Others said that might explain how screwed up I was at that time, leaving college to join the USMC as an infantryman at the height of the Vietnam War. What was I thinking?

I think it all started back in about 1963 (my junior year in high school), when the war in Vietnam was becoming a news item and students were becoming aware of it. There was quite a bit of talk about it on the evening news with Walter Cronkite. The insertion of the Green Berets into Vietnam had aroused an interest in jungle warfare, and I had foolishly written in my high school yearbook that my "silly ambition" was to learn jungle guerrilla warfare. I wasn't thinking clearly in those days, and many say I have never gotten over that malady.

Being from a family that said I had to go to college or I'd be considered a failure, I never really seriously considered a military option, but being from a family that never said *why* I should go to college, I never set any goals or thought about what I wanted to study. So I enrolled at the University of Minnesota in Minneapolis and spent three years learning a little about a lot but never much about anything. I never declared a major, as I was never seriously interested in anything specific. I was half stepping through life, with no goals and no direction.

I remember the day clearly. I was driving home from the U of M campus during the spring quarter in 1967. I heard an appealing advertisement that made the Marine Corps life sound exciting, glamorous, and fetching. The radio stated that there could be no better decision than to stop by the Marine Corps office on Broadway and discuss all the wonderful choices and options available for enlisting today. Besides, they had a "special plan" then, where you could join up with a buddy and go to boot camp together. My life at that time was anything but exciting, glamorous, and fetching.

Well, as it happened (happenstance was just beginning to show its fickle head), I was just then approaching Broadway from the south, heading north toward home, and I thought that it couldn't hurt to stop in and see what they had to offer. Since high school and the beginning of the buildup in Vietnam, I remembered that I had always wanted to learn about "jungle warfare" and Green Beret life.

After all, I was not doing all that well in school. I hadn't declared a major. I hadn't a clue what I wanted to do for the rest of my life. I didn't even have a girlfriend anymore. I thought I might need a break from what I was doing. I'd just been treading water, marking time. Maybe it was time to do something constructive. Besides, it wouldn't take long to see what they offered, and then I'd head home. Nothing ventured, nothing gained. I'd consider what they said … later.

The recruiting sergeant was a nice guy, friendly as a pickpocket. He had me signed up for a two-year stint on the buddy plan with Gary Ehn in about fifteen minutes, maybe thirty minutes tops. I knew Gary as a coworker at Shoppers' City grocery and department store, where we both were carry out boys together back in our high school days. That had been two or three years ago. I hadn't seen him since, but I remembered him. It seemed he had also stopped by this same recruiting office recently.

Gary was a Minnesota boy all the way—modest, strong, good-looking, friendly, and a hard worker. He always did his share and never complained. He also went to Patrick Henry High School but was a few years younger than I, so I didn't know him well, other than from Shoppers' City.

We joined a bunch of other Minnesota boys, mostly from around the Twin Cities area. We were all inducted as a group at the same time on national TV at a Minnesota Twins ball game in Minneapolis on June 28, 1967. We were called the "Twins Platoon" because the Minnesota Twins Ball Club sponsored us. There were about 150 new recruits divided into two platoons. Gary Ehn was assigned to the other platoon, but I did see him once while in boot camp. And we did travel on the same plane to boot camp, so strictly speaking, we did go to boot camp together.

On that special day, we all watched the first eight innings of the ball game. It was an exciting evening watching local heroes Rod Carew, Harmon Killebrew, Zoilo Versalles, Jim Kaat, Dave Boswell, and Tony Oliva seemingly playing just for us.

Then those in charge decided it was time to leave—at the top of the ninth inning! Dave Boswell (I think it was) had struck out thirteen already and was having a great game. I couldn't believe we were leaving! How could this be happening? I never did find out how that game ended. Welcome to the marines!

We arrived in San Diego, California, at three or four in the morning after a long and uncomfortable flight in a four-engine prop plane. Old orange school buses picked us up at an empty terminal at Lindberg Field. They ferried us around to the other side of the airport, where Marine Corps Recruit Depot (MCRD) awaited us. I didn't know where I was, other than I was in a big city.

I was as unprepared for Marine Corps boot camp as I had been for college back in Minnesota. Planning ahead and making well-thought-out decisions had never yet been one of my better attributes. I was a born impulse buyer, not a planner.

Off-loading the buses, we milled around outside the base. A big cement wall with two wooden wide-swinging doors kept us outside. Large fluorescent floodlights lit up our holding pen in a stark ghostly light.

At the time, it reminded me of a medieval castle wall meant to protect those on the inside from things on the outside—but maybe it was meant to keep things on the inside of the walls inside those walls, keeping them from getting out. I wondered what the more likely answer was. The other thing of note was many yellow footprints painted on the concrete.

It gradually became ominously quiet as people stopped talking and stopped speculating about what was next on the agenda. The stillness became evident, and an eerie spookiness settled over us. Apprehension overtook us all as we warily searched for what might be coming next. We began to notice that standing tall up on the top of the wall was a large marine, watching us derisively. This marine commanded our attention without speaking. He was dressed perfectly in pressed fatigues, spit-polished black shoes, and his Smokey the Bear drill instructor hat.

He had our attention. There wasn't a sound in the pen. He was the most ominous-looking physically fit person I had ever seen in person. I was sure he could crush a normal man simply by shaking his hand. I don't remember the entire speech, but Sergeant Lewis informed us that he was now our drill instructor and that we were in his charge. From now on, we would do everything he said, without question, and we would learn to do it right—the Marine Corps way! We would forget our weak, lazy civilian ways and would learn to become Marine Corps warriors.

We would address him as "Sir, yes sir." He would address us as "maggots, pukes, and scum."

This is the night I received my Marine Corp name, "Basteen." My real name is Bastien, pronounced BAST-CHEN, or BASS-CHEN, if you want the French version. When our new instructor ("Sir, yes, sir") did a role call to ensure everyone had arrived, he mispronounced my name as BASS-TEEN.

I decided very quickly that he did not look like the kind of guy who would appreciate being corrected at our first meeting, especially by a brand-new maggot, puke, scum recruit, so I graciously let it slide. The name stuck with me the rest of my days in the USMC. That's what everyone called me from then on. So what was the big deal? "Basteen" is just as good as "Bastchen" *or* "Basschen."

Boot camp was everything you might ever have imagined about it. Three drill instructors alternated turns, for thirteen weeks, at breaking us down and then building us back up their way. It was physical and psychological harassment meant to wear us down to the point where they could start over and build us back up, becoming physically and psychologically fit, real marines.

The routine was early rising; marching; PT (physical training); learning about the Marine Corps environment, history, and family; what it means to make a mistake (not good); weapons training and education; following orders, dress codes, and becoming disciplined … All good stuff.

In the mess hall, you ate everything they put on the tray. That's where I learned to like beef liver. I didn't have a choice in the matter. Some things I never did learn to like, but I ate them anyway. That wasn't a choice either. It was good training for later days. In the evenings, we had the traditional three minutes to shave, shit, and shower. It was mandatory that you shave and shower. Sometimes, if the DI was in a good mood, we would get mail call.

The first time we had mail call, we got the rules. You read what is readable and then throw it in the trash. *Or*, if it is not readable, you eat it. That very night, I received a thirteen-page letter from Neil Brodin, a best friend from high school who had preceded me into the service by a few weeks by joining the army. His long, rambling letter explained all the reasons he could think of why I should *not* join any military service right then. Hmm … nice timing.

As I read it, I was wondering what quirk of luck could have caused that letter to arrive just *after* I started boot camp rather than arriving at my home a few weeks earlier. Was this also luck, chance, or happenstance? Over the next several months, I would come to ponder more and more about how those things interacted and related to our lives.

Boot camp was extended for some reason unknown to me, but near the end, we had acquired a smidgen of respect from the DIs. As we became more proficient in doing things their way, we did fewer knuckle push-ups and were not called "maggots" quite as frequently. Occasionally, they even held what amounted to "fireside chats" with us. Sergeant Lewis, Sergeant Taylor, and Staff Sergeant Jenkins shared their Vietnam stories and advice. Sergeant Taylor shared his advice to "make acquaintances but never make friends." I wondered about that. I would later come to understand why he gave that advice.

★★★

The big day had finally arrived. It was graduation day. When the ceremony ended, we had become marines. We were no longer maggots, pukes, and scum. We were "real marines." We could be addressed as "Private So-and-So." Our families and friends were there to congratulate us, along with our proud drill Instructors, who had created another batch of Marine Corps warriors from the lazy, sloppy, and weak civilian population of retards they had been assigned. We all stood proud!

The celebration lasted an hour or two, and then most of us boarded buses bound for Camp Pendleton and advanced infantry training. This would be our introduction to real warfare and weapons. We would learn the skills necessary to be a marine infantry rifleman. We were excited about the new challenge and yet a little nervous, apprehensive about living up to the standards of real marines. We were at least starting off well, looking our best in fresh "starchy green fatigues," soft cover hats, and polished tall black leather boots. We had our seabags full of everything we owned in the world. And we were ready and anxious to become marine infantry riflemen.

Turning off Highway 5 in Southern California, we entered Camp Pendleton, but it was nowhere near any base civilization. We were rumbling down a narrow twisting dirt road bordered by cactus and other desert plants. There were *no* signs of civilization, and I had *no* idea where I was. We bumped along for a while and then stopped in the middle of nowhere. We off-loaded from the buses and picked up our heavy, bulky, and cumbersome seabags.

A single solitary marine sergeant who met us there said to follow him. He was *not* wearing a Smokey the Bear hat, so I knew this was not boot camp anymore. He had no seabag, so I thought we must be close. Well, that was wrong. We straggled down that dirt road at least another mile or two, seabags slung over our shoulders.

The temperatures were in the eighties or nineties. The dust of the road and desert was pervasive. It was a hot day in the desert. By the time we got to the buildings, we looked as if we had just swum across the sandpit back at MCRD, as we had done several times in boot camp. We were a ragged-ass mess, all of us. I was thinking, *Well, so much for the nice fresh starchies and lookin' good.*

The sergeant stopped and jumped up on a big rock, perfectly formed for addressing a raggedy-ass bunch of first-timers to AIT. I noticed a few barracks buildings not too far away. I'll not forget his first words to us: "Some of you think you are marines now that you've graduated MCRD. Some of you think you have earned respect. But out here, you will be starting over. Out here, the only difference between here and boot camp is that out here … you can die and nobody will know."

We spent several weeks in different weapons classes, including a mock prisoner-of-war camp, where we were able to escape and then had to sneak past "enemy" watch posts carefully to get back to "friendly" territory. When we arrived back in friendly territory, we were each given a poncho. It was a cold and wet November night, but we were told to find anywhere on the ground where we wanted to sleep for the rest of the night. I couldn't believe the inhumanity of this, but I played the game, believing this could never happen again in real life!

After completion of AIT, we had earned a week off. I returned home and spent time with Mom, Dad, my brother, and friends. One of the highlights that I remember was a last golf session with another good high school buddy, Randy Moskalik. We decided to play Theodore Wirth Golf Course, in Minneapolis, just one more time, for old times' sake. Little did I suspect that he had squirreled away several six-packs into his golf bag. Rules for the day were that we couldn't tee off from any hole until we finished a beer. I don't remember if we finished the first nine, let alone the entire round. I think this was his way of saying that we were friends—and goodbye. We both knew the unspoken truth, that there was some chance that we might not ever see each other again.

The fun times ended, and I returned to Camp Pendleton. Those going to Vietnam assembled, and we were taken to El Toro Air Base, where we would board a plane the next day for Okinawa and then go on to Vietnam. There was an old gunnery sergeant in charge of this group. He was a smallish man, seemingly past retirement age, and he certainly didn't have the demeanor or the physique of a take charge marine sergeant. He looked more like he should be playing cello in the symphony.

At El Toro, they herded us rowdies into an enclosure that was really the camp prison. The two barracks buildings and yard were surrounded by chain-link fence and concertina wire on top of that.

The buildings were two stories each. There were sleeping quarters on each floor, with metal frame bunks and mattresses. There were no sheets, blankets, or pillows. At the end of the building were showers and the head.

Somebody had smuggled booze of some kind into the enclosure, and that night some of the guys became a little rowdy. Actually, for many of them, it was a full-scale riot. In their drunken wildness, they were throwing mattresses out the second-story window, running around fighting, and blathering things like, "What are they gonna do, send me to Nam?"

I sat outside against the only tree in the yard. I sat in fine-grain dusty dirt. It felt like ash under the leafless tree. There was no grass. The yard surrounding the barracks was bare. I watched the riot and the poor gunny trying to take back control. Much later, everyone settled down and tried to find a mattress. The lights were out except where they shined on the fences. In the morning, we boarded buses to the terminal. I don't remember having any breakfast.

I saw it arrive from the east. Maneuvering to land, the four-engine Boeing 707 oil burner turned base to final in front of the mountains a few miles out. It landed, returning a batch of soldiers to the real world and picked us up for our trip to an unreal world. It was quiet on board. Half the guys were still hungover, and half were contemplating what lay ahead. Not knowing what lay ahead, I started trying to imagine what it would be. There was no way to imagine the sights, sounds, or encounters that were to come.

I didn't know it then, but after thirteen months of combat infantry experience in Vietnam, it becomes one of those periods in your life that never goes away, is never entirely forgotten, and subconsciously affects all the remaining days of your life one way or another.

The adventure had begun!

CHAPTER 6

ARRIVAL

Looking out the side window, I had seen nothing but cloud or water for hours, and it wasn't until nearly touchdown that I got my first glance at the place. We arrived in Da Nang, Vietnam, sometime in the morning of December 2, 1967. And then too quickly to see anything important, we were on the ground, rolling past F4-Phantoms and their open-air but individualized enclosures separating one from each other; OV-10 Broncos, which were new to me but awesome rugged-looking twin turboprops built for observation and fighting; tanks and jeeps; and miscellaneous trucks and flatbeds carrying weapons or cargo to and from the cargo planes. I saw a long line of cheap-looking quickly built buildings that appear to be temporary maintenance hangars and offices. I also saw many sandbags, walls of them stacked high up to a man's shoulders around and between buildings and jet enclosures. This place was seriously prepared for attack.

The frail old gunnery sergeant led us out single file and down the airstairs. He looked as if he had done this before and knew what he was doing. He seemed suddenly in his element and had credibility in the command role. His steps were quick and sure. He led us over to a yellow line on the tarmac and commanded us to line up along the length of it and to stay behind it. He now sounded strong and confident.

My first impression stepping out of the 707 aircraft door and onto the airstair steps was that it was like stepping into a steam bath. It was hot, steamy, and muggy. It smelled like a locker room. My glasses started to fog. I could feel a stinky workout sweat under my armpits. Everyone else was sweating too. The old Gunny seemed immune to it. That confirmed it for me; he had been here before—probably knew what he was doing too.

No time to dwell on that, though. Follow single file and line up along the yellow line. The line stretched for a long way. There were probably eighty or ninety of us side by side. I was about in the middle.

A few people were talking quietly, but otherwise we were just waiting to be told what to do and where to go. The guy next to me leaned over toward me slightly and kind of whispered, "Whatever you do, don't go to Kilo 3/5."

"Why not?" I asked.

Speaking secretly just to me now, he said, "Those guys are bad. They just blew up their first sergeant."

"Huh? What do you mean, 'they just blew up their first sergeant'?"

"I mean, somebody just rolled a hand grenade under his cot and blew him up a few nights ago."

I wanted to ask him more about all this—like, how did he know that already? We just got here. But just then, somebody exited one of the temporary offices and walked out toward us. Something would be happening. He walked with authority and looked purposeful, but he was obviously just an office gopher corporal doing his office job. I reminded myself not to go to Kilo 3/5 (as if I would have a choice).

The corporal squinted his eyes to slits in the bright sun. He was clearly in a hurry to get back to his air-conditioned office. Without saying a word, he started at the far end of the line and walked down the line. He seemed to be counting. When he got to me, he stopped and raised his hand above my head. Then he dropped it down between me and the guy next to me, who had just given me the warning about not going to Kilo 3/5. He divided the line right in two, directly between us.

This was the first instance of happenstance that I encountered in Vietnam. There would be more.

He then used his other hand to signal to everyone on that side of his arm, and he yelled so everyone could hear, "Everyone on this side goes to Lima Company, three/five!" Then he signaled to everybody on my side of his arm, and he yelled so everyone could hear, "Everyone on this side is going to Kilo Company, three-five!"

The guy with the warning looked at me, smiled, and said "Good luck."

He turned away and followed his line to the trucks bound for Lima Company. I turned and followed the rest of my line out to the trucks bound for Kilo Company, wherever that was. I was last in line, and it would not be the only time I was last in a line. Actually, we were all bound for the same battalion area, except I was going to Kilo Company when we got there. We loaded into the back end of trucks and started out on the journey.

Da Nang was no large modern metropolitan city. Once we left the air base, it seemed more of a shantytown from what I could see. The streets we traveled on were all busy and lined with one- or two-story shops covered with corrugated tin roofs. There were a lot of bikes, mopeds, and motorbikes but few large vehicles like our convoy of trucks. Most of the people were dressed in pajama-like silky pants and tops and were wearing conical straw hats. It was hot, noisy, and busy. They seemed to be bustling and hustling here and there.

We left the city for the open quiet spaces on dirt roads, going into jungle forests and alongside rice paddies. We passed through several small villages that had no two-story buildings. The roads sometimes became narrow one-lane roads, with jungle right up to the edges. I was thinking this looked like dangerous country to me and we hadn't even been issued weapons yet. How safe were we?

After a while, we lumbered into the 3/5 Battalion compound. The front gate opened, and our trucks drove in, split up, and went their separate ways. It seemed to be a large base. Our truck took us to our new home area. We disembarked and stood in another line. A few guys showed up. One guy had a clipboard. He read two or three names off a list and directed them to go with one of the old guys he'd brought along with him. He did this several times. Off they went to their new homes and jobs.

Finally, I was the only one left, and I was with the clipboard guy. He said, "Come with me." We started walking past a bunch of buildings (hooches) built with cement foundations in order to support half-height walls of plywood. Wooden posts held up the tent-top ceiling. The plywood walls went up to about the height of one's navel, and then there was netting between the lower wood part and the tent ceiling. These would be our homes. They housed ten or twelve marines each and were equipped with cots. Screened-in hooches with a real door and a floor—luxuries I'd not see often again.

Clipboard Guy and I walked past some of these, and at one I noticed that the entire corner seemed to have been blown out by some sort of explosion. "What's this?" I asked.

He replied to me matter-of-factly, "Somebody rolled a hand grenade under the first sergeant's cot a few nights ago."

I was stunned. Not only was it true that some marine intentionally blew up another marine but also that the guy in line with me at the air base had known about it. How in the world …? I realized right then and there that Vietnam was a nasty and dangerous place, not to be taken lightly.

We arrived at a hooch farther on down the line. Clipboard Guy said, "This is yours. Stay here."

"Where is everybody?"

He said, "They're out on patrol. They'll be back in a while." Then he turned and headed back to wherever he came from. I was alone.

I sat on a cot in the far corner, away from the door. It didn't seem to be occupied, and I waited, wondering who would be coming back later. There was nobody else in the hooch. There were several cots, some with gear on them. I had no idea what to do, where to go, or what any of the procedures were around here. I stayed put as directed.

As I sat there all alone, knowing nothing about where I was, what I should do, or what was going to happen, I realized that I was now in Vietnam and was just as unprepared for it as I had been unprepared for college and the marines at boot camp. It didn't seem that this was the place to be unprepared.

After what seemed an eternity, I saw through the screened door several marines walking my way. There were five of them. They were dirty, sweaty, mean-looking weapon-carrying grunts like you'd see in the movies. They looked as if they'd just as soon gouge your eyeballs out as talk to you.

The screen door busted open, and the first four walked in, found cots, dropped their gear, and plopped down to rest, never acknowledging me in the corner. The last guy stood in the doorway and looked at me. He was a tall marine, soaked with sweat, still holding his M16 rifle. He was looking right at me, eyeball to eyeball, and said in a loud, booming voice, "Who's from Minnesota?"

I looked around. The only people in the hooch were his four buddies and me. I figured he was talking to me, so I raised my hand like a schoolkid. However, I was confused. How did he know it already? News seemed to travel fast here in Vietnam, that was for sure. I didn't know how he knew where I was from.

His face loosened up and he smiled a big grin. "I'm from North High School in Minneapolis," he said, walking over to me. "Where are you from?"

Whew, at least he wasn't going to shoot me. "I went to Patrick Henry."

It was as if we were long-lost buddies who had just found each other after years apart. He sat down on my cot, and we covered growing up on the north side of Minneapolis, going to schools only a few miles apart, sports, girls, and so forth.

Suddenly, I was here and had friends. Well, I had one friend and four others I'd get to know soon enough. Cronen was actually like a big, skinny Santa Claus, with a hearty laugh, friendly as a teddy bear, and I felt that he would do anything for a friend. Let him gain 150 pounds and give him a red snow cap and he was the real deal Santa.

Louisiana was the machine gunner carrying the M60 with both hands hanging down to the waist and two belts of M60 ammunition crisscrossed across his soldiers like Pancho Villa. He looked and acted like the bad guy in the movies—quiet, a loner, and wearing a mean scowl. I'm pretty sure he came from somewhere in the state of Louisiana.

Larry Brown was a rifleman carrying two M60 belts plus several grenades and an M16 rifle. Brown was from Franklin, Kentucky, and was a great shot with a rifle. He seemingly didn't get along well with the law, and that probably was why he was here.

Hencke was another rifleman clone of Brown, carrying the same weapons and gear. Hencke was a young kid just off the farm in Iowa. Wilson carried the LAAW (light antitank assault weapon), a small shoulder-fired rocket). I'd find out later that Wilson had just arrived recently too and would eventually become my squad leader in weapons platoon.

Steve Cronen was squad leader for this group of misfits and my new best friend. I was the outsider being welcomed as a friend as well as the new replacement. This was a valuable friend to have who may make a life-death difference in the future, as they all are.

Cronen, Brown, Wilson, and the others accepted me, the FNG (fucking new guy), and they showed me the ropes … mostly where the showers and head were located, where the mess hall was, but most importantly where to get rid of these ugly recruit depot fatigues and boots for the new in-style camouflage utilities and jungle boots. Nobody wanted to be seen with somebody wearing high-top black leather boots. You were not even here until you had jungle utilities and boots. It was as if you were invisible or advertising that you were a FNG.

That over, the next thing was to get a weapon. We went to the armory, and I checked out an M16 rifle. They took me to the practice range. I fired off a few rounds and signed it out as mine. I was now "certified" as a Marine Corps rifleman, ready for patrol, night ambush—all those fun things.

Nothing happened for a few days other than trudging through the red mud back and forth to the mess hall in the mornings for breakfast and evenings for supper. Cronen's squad had been given a short respite. They didn't mind, but I was actually a little anxious to see what it is all about. We just waited.

There was an artillery battery on base. Fire missions were called in every night from guys out in the bush. The booms and bangs were so loud and so frequent that it was hard to sleep. Actually, it was earth-shattering for the first few nights. Then I grew accustomed to it. I didn't even hear it anymore. That is, until one night when we all were awakened by a tremendously loud explosion not two or three hooches away. A high explosive artillery round fell short. It landed right smack-dab into a barracks tent full with several sleeping marines. It killed everybody in the hooch. That misfire created several more names for the Vietnam Memorial Wall, a needless loss. I subconsciously started my "close calls" list in my head. That was number one. I wondered how many would I get.

Steve Cronen in Phu Bai just after returning from recovery after being WIA. This was not what he'd looked like when I first met him at the old 3/5 area. Here, he had shaved, taken a shower, had clean utilities, had been fed at the mess hall, and was feeling good. It was quite a different sight when I first saw him.

This is to show the "big, skinny Santa Claus" nature of Cronen. His hearty laugh warmed up any cold night or tense situation.

I'm showing Steve at Phu Bai because I don't have any pictures of the old 3/5 area and I at least want to show a little bit of "the rear."

CHAPTER 7

THE 3/5 BATTALION AREA

Something happened. I didn't know when, why, or how it happened. Somehow, Cronen found out we were going out on a platoon-wide patrol today. I discovered that he knew this because he briefed the rest of us in the hooch. Somewhere along the line, I had missed "Communications 101" in Vietnam. I knew I had to figure out how everyone else seemed to know stuff I needed to know. Why was I the last to find out anything?

We were to be on a day patrol only, so we didn't need overnight gear like ponchos or poncho liners. He did say to bring lots of water. I had a utility belt on which I could hang up to four water canteens and my gas mask. We wouldn't need the flak jackets, but we had to wear the hard hats. I strapped on two bandoliers of M16 magazines, several grenades, and grabbed my M16. Decked out in new camouflage utilities and jungle boots, I was ready and raring to get this show on the road. This was my first patrol, and I was excited.

We walked out the gate into a rising sun. It was already hot and humid. The mud was still soft and squishy as we walked down the road. I was with the Third Platoon, and now I was with the Third Squad and being the new guy in town I was also now "tail-end Charlie," last guy in the line. Somehow, another rookie had joined us, and since Haycraft had a few days of seniority on me, he was second to the last in this parade. Haycraft and I brought up the rear.

Soon we turned off the road and started our trek into the jungle forest and across the streams. My socks got soaked, but my good boots were squishing the water out with every step. Then we started up some hills. As we climbed the hills, the land dried out. We found the crest line of those hills and followed it. We were walking along a trail. I couldn't tell if it had been there permanently, used by the locals or possibly the NVA infiltrating the area, or if it was just made by the other forty guys walking in front of me. Alongside the trail grew tall weeds and bushes that reached up to about our waists. On either side of the crest line, these weeds and bushes extended for forty or fifty yards each way, out to a tree line that spread out as forest on a hillside back down to the flat lands and rice paddies below.

We walked for about two hours, and it was quite hot under the blazing sun. The sky was a bright blue and the green forest of trees on both sides of the ridge made a colorful picture while we followed the brown trail to wherever we were going. I had no idea where we were going, and nobody had informed me of anything. I was just following the guy in front of me. I had no idea what was going on.

I could soon tell that I was not in shape for this and not ready for this. I was sweating like a sponge being squeezed to mop the floor, and my nice new cammies were dark with sweat. I had already drunk one full canteen of water. I was fatigued, and I wanted to take a nap. Haycraft didn't look like he was doing much better than I was. That was some consolation anyway. I was not the only one.

Somebody up front finally decided that it was a good time to take a break, which Haycraft and I desperately needed. Maybe they were getting tired too. Anyway, for them it meant sit down for a few minutes, have a gulp of water, and open a C ration can of pineapples in juice, or something like that.

For Haycraft and me, it meant fall down flat on our backs and immediately fall asleep in the warm sun and soft grasses off the trail.

Sometime later (I have no idea how much time later), my eyes popped open and I was wide-awake. I was suddenly panic-stricken with a thought that something was wrong. I sat up and looked around, especially down the trail ahead. I didn't see anyone or anything. Haycraft suddenly popped up from the grasses a few feet ahead. His eyes were as round as silver dollars, and he had that same panic expression on his face.

There was nobody here! We were alone; we had been left behind. Where did they go? On our very first day in the field, we had gotten separated from our group. How could this be? When they got up to leave, didn't they at least look around to see if everybody was with them? It seemed not. So the rookies (the FNGs) were left behind.

Neither of us had any idea how long we had slept or where the platoon went. We just knew that we had better find them. We jumped up and started hauling ass down the path in the direction we had been going, hoping to catch up to them, hoping that's where they went.

As I ran, I was frightened that instead of finding our marines, we'd run into a VC or NVA position or that they would be waiting for us in ambush. I was also frightened that somebody would find out that I fell asleep on duty. It didn't matter that we were on break, that the sun was warm, that the grasses were soft, that I was so tired already—that I feel asleep. You couldn't do that. I was both embarrassed and scared.

I didn't know what Haycraft was thinking. I didn't even care what he was thinking. We were both running as if we were embarrassed and scared. If we just kept running, we'd have to catch up to our guys. That was a great idea until we got to a branch in the trail, one trail to the right and one trail to the left. "Shit, which way did they go?"

If I had been born an Indian tracker, I might have been able to tell, but being born a city boy, I couldn't tell you which path forty marines had just taken. So, we branched left and kept running.

Finally, we came to another trail. It seemed our trail ended right there, where it ran into a more major main trail. We were standing there at the intersection of these trails, in thick forest, trying to decide which way to go when the point man from the platoon walked into the intersection from the trail to our right. He calmly said, "I should have blown you two idiots away, but I heard you talking. The NVA wouldn't be talking. How'd you get in front of us?"

I simply said that we got too far behind and then took the wrong branch back there. I was so relieved that I almost started laughing or crying hysterically, but I held it together. So did Haycraft.

He simply muttered something about FNGs and continued on his way, with the rest of the platoon following in step, eyeing us quizzically but nobody saying a thing. When the last guy went by, we fell into position at the end as if we knew what we were doing. I asked Haycraft what "FNG" meant, and he replied "Fucking new guy."

As we headed home, I wondered how Haycraft knew what FNG meant. He'd only been in the country a couple of days longer than I had. He hadn't been to any classes that I hadn't. I wanted my money back. Those classes back in the States hadn't taught me anything. The rest of the day was uneventful.

We got back to the battalion area and ate supper in the mess hall. I asked Cronen if we were going out again tomorrow. He said, "Not in the day but we'll be going out on a night ambush."

I spent the next day cleaning my M16, getting five or six bandoliers of M16 magazines ready, loading up all my water canteens and assembling everything I owned. I was ready. Cronen said to me, on our way through the red mud to the mess hall for early supper, that all I needed was one canteen, one bandolier of M16 magazines, a few grenades, no pack, and a soft cover. We were going light and tight.

Just after sunset, at twilight, we assembled and checked that we were all here. We were all here (physically at least), and I was placed, once again, as tail-end Charlie, last in line. This time there were only four of us, and I did not intend to be separated from them. I would keep them in sight. So it was Steve in the lead, Brown, Missouri, and then me. Missouri had an M16, not the M60 this time. We were light loaded and stealthy.

Everything was tied down tight. There was no clanging or banging. I might have been a new Cherrie, but I was proud that I was tightly packed as everybody else. The only noise was our footsteps crunching along the gravel road. The only sight was our silhouettes in the fading twilight.

We followed the gravel road down to a highway (highway meaning paved road). Then we turned and walked along the road until it was almost full dark. There was no traffic. Actually, it was deserted and very quiet. Even the village we walked past was deserted. Nobody was stirring.

As soon as it became fully dark, Cronen led us down off the raised roadway into the jungle and rice paddies below at normal ground level. We paralleled the raised road, keeping low so that we couldn't be seen from the other side. We walked until the village we passed was well behind. Then everyone sat down and leaned against the dirt embankment, which was built to keep the road six or more feet above floods. We'd wait there until we were sure nobody was watching from the far tree line.

It was very dark, but I could see the glow from a full moon beginning to rise from behind the forest trees on the other side of this large open field. Steve whispered, "We better go set up before that moon rises."

We did a crouching walk out to the middle of this big field that was littered with large round mounds. There was plenty of space between mounds and plenty of large bushy plants growing in between. Cronen found a nice group of bushes that could surround us for cover, and that's where we set up. Steve and Brown faced the highway and Missouri and I faced the tree line. We would have two-hour watches and two-hour sleeps. Two guys were awake all the time. It was late December and the nights were long. It might have been a twelve-hour night.

I got the first watch, and Missouri was settling in a bed of weeds. I asked him, "What are these mounds?"

He whispered, "Burial mounds."

Great! We were set up for a night ambush in a cemetery. That was as spooky as I wanted to see. Actually, it wasn't so bad, as I later found out that the poor in Vietnam often buried their dead in these burial mounds right in the rice paddies and fields and continued to plant and grow crops around them. In this huge field were many burial mounds. The problem with these burial mounds was that they obstructed vision to the far tree line and to the highway. There were only a few avenues of clear vision past the mounds.

It had been very quiet and still. The mosquitoes were buzzing in my ears, flying up my nose, and landing on my face. I couldn't afford to swat them because the movement and the noise might alert someone out there about our ambush. I made a mental note to find mosquito repellent before the next op.

The moon was now rising above the treetops and casting moon glow shadows of the burial mounds and other plants across the field. I had to stay low, below the tops of these plants, because a sitting marine could cast a very recognizable silhouette shadow. So I was on my stomach propped up on my elbows, not very comfortably.

It was too quiet and too still. I didn't even hear mosquitoes anymore. I was watching the tree line and everything in between through the open areas of the burial mounds. Then I saw a shadow move. At least something caught my attention. I looked again, and it seemed to be crawling. My heartrate climbed to about 220, and I thought the thumping would wake everybody up. I couldn't believe it. First night ambush on my first night watch and I was seeing a VC or NVA sneaking up on us? Should I shoot? Should I throw a grenade? Did I really see that?

I figured it was so close that I'd better throw a grenade. I grabbed one off my belt and pulled the pin, ready to lob it out there just as soon as I saw this guy. Wait, wait, wait … wait until you're sure.

I waited, but I didn't see any more movement. Where was he? Was he behind that big bush or was he going behind that burial mound? Shit. I didn't see anything. Did he move while I was getting the grenade?

Shit, shit, shit … Now I was scared. He was probably right behind that burial mound over there, ready to throw a grenade on me. I had better warn Louisiana. I didn't want to talk, so I started kicking him with my boot until he rolled over and said, "What?"

I whispered that I thought I saw somebody crawling across the ground out there. I pointed between two burial mounds.

He said, "What did you see?"

I whispered that I saw his shadow moving across the ground.

Louisiana looked, saw nothing, and said, "There's nothing out there. It's your imagination."

He rolled over and went back to sleep. I didn't know what to think. I looked some more, and I didn't see anything either. Maybe it was my imagination. I'd be awake all night tonight thinking about it, making sure.

Now what do I do with this live grenade in my hand with the pin already pulled out? Should I throw it or put the pin back in? Can you even put the pin back in once it has been pulled? Now I was sweating nervous sweat, not workout sweat. I decided that everybody would be really pissed if I threw the grenade and then we had to move and start all over again, after I gave away our position, so I decided to put the pin back into the grenade.

But where did I put the pin? I frantically began searching my shirt pocket, my cover, and the ground around me. Luckily, I found the pin and carefully reinserted it. I made sure the end was bent so that the pin couldn't decide to back out again on its own. I didn't shut my eyes for the rest of the night.

At first light, Cronen said, "Let's go have some breakfast." We got up, headed back to the highway, and walked back to the battalion area. No big deal; it was a quiet night. Along the way, I asked Louisiana how he knew there was nobody out there and said that I hadn't seen anything.

Louisiana explained in a fatherly voice, a teacher telling the FNG, that if you wanted to see something at night you didn't look directly at it, you looked off to the side of it. That's because of where the rods and cones are located in the eye. Rods see well at night, but they are located away from the focal point. Cones see well during the day, and they are all located at the focal point of the eye. This is good for daytime vision. At night, you need rods to see better, so you use peripheral vision and do not look directly at what you want to see.

★★★

After my first day patrol and my first night ambush, we fell into a routine of about two or three day patrols in small squads, followed by a night patrol or ambush. It seemed to have been the new normal, and all the other squads were doing it too. It was impossible to go out without getting feet wet. The area was crisscrossed with streams, and there were very few roads, which we avoided anyway. The idea was to search for Charlie and surprise him by approaching from an unsuspecting place.

We invariably walked down a stream with water up to our knees simply to approach a possible enemy area from an unsuspecting and hidden view. Those streams did not seem to be freshwater mountain-type streams but appeared muddy gray, similar to what I imagined the Florida Everglades to be. At least it was easier walking down a stream than it was hacking our way through the dense jungle undergrowth. Wilson and I seemed to be together on several of these, and I got somebody to snap a picture of us slogging through the water on one of them.

We traveled lightly, no flak jackets but always with the hard hat steel helmets. On these patrols, we were riflemen and didn't bring any of the heavy weapons. Fortunately, there was little action. I had started a journal on a spiral notebook when I got there, but so far, it had been empty. I tossed it in the trash.

We did occasionally go on an overnighter. Charlie traveled mostly at night. Our job was to intercept and stop him. We were out somewhere, and I had no idea where it was. It was night. We had stopped. I was flat on my back, lying on the jungle floor and watching the stars. Suddenly, I sensed movement down by my foot. I raised my head slightly to see what it was and to see if I truly saw anything at all.

I did see something. I saw a snake slither past my foot on the inside of my legs. Then he went over my leg, past my arm, and continued into the jungle. He was going somewhere in a hurry and he was not interested in me, thank goodness.

Back in the battalion area, I received a letter from my old best friend from high school days. Neil wrote to say that he was off to Washington, DC, for some spit and polish, Old Guard duty, which was a pretty big deal, and I wondered how he managed that. At the end of his letter, he notified me that "my" Nicky was getting married on one of the days coming up later in December. I forget which day it was.

Nina (Nicky) was my girlfriend back in high school days. Neil and I both saw her on the second day of senior high. She was a junior and had the job of going to each classroom to gather the attendance sheets. She entered Rodney Rays's algebra class and walked across the front of the room to pick up his sheet. I decided that I had to meet her, which I actually was able to do. I don't remember how I found the courage to do that, but I did. I have only felt that way about two women in my entire life, Nicky and my current wife, Carol, whom I have managed to stay married to for over thirty years.

Nina and I soon went "steady" for the rest of the year, going to movies, events, and finally the senior and junior proms. It was a great time, and I was happy. She too, I thought. But then, as graduation day came, she told me she wanted me to be free to go out with other girls. "I will be going to college, and I should be free to meet other people," she said.

I argued that I was only going to the U of M, which was still in Minneapolis, and that I wasn't going anywhere. But she insisted.

I think it was really that *she* wanted to be free—or maybe her folks wanted to see if I was serious or not. Anyway, I was crushed and never got the nerve to call her or ask her out again.

On the day that she was to get married, Cronen's squad and I were out on another night ambush. We came back at first light as per usual, but instead of going to the mess hall, I wandered over to the base chapel.

I have never been religiously inclined, but for some reason, it seemed right. I sat down in one of the pews to reflect on what might have been. I sat for a long while. Then I suddenly prayed for her and for them together to have a great life full of happiness.

I realized then that her absence had been an emptiness in my life for the last three years, and that emptiness possibly was one of the reasons I had never developed plans for anything and was drifting aimlessly.

I imagined that getting this news from Neil was very much like the other guys getting their "Dear John" letters from a wife or girlfriend. At first, it was a kick in the gut. Many of those guys went berserk, like stand-up-in-a-firefight berserk. However, for me, it became a liberating thing, a closure event. I suddenly felt relieved and ready to move on. It was a turning point. I was past Nicky. And I was proud of myself for sincerely wishing them the best.

Then, probably because I was in a chapel, my thoughts moved on to *Why am I here?* What was I doing here, anyway? I realized that I was about to embark on a year or more of searching for bad guys and trying to kill them. I asked myself, "How moral is that?"

I wrestled with justifications, stated and implied reasons for all this, and my obligations to my country and fellow marines here with me now. There were so many arguments for and against. Nobody was saying it, but we were here and Charlie was trying to kill or maim us to get us to leave. The unsaid truth was that we needed to do it first and we needed to be better, as it was for our own protection, simply so we could go home.

Whether we should be there or not, whether we should be doing what we were doing, and whether it was morally okay or not was too much for me to consider right then; I didn't have the will to consider these questions at that point. I saw that this could become an overwhelming moral dilemma, and I didn't have the time or energy for that. I decided to put the questions aside and reconsider my morality later, when I returned home. I was glad for the decision, and I tucked the concerns away for another day. I had now happily moved on past two emotional blockades. Maybe I should visit a chapel again.

★★★

Over breakfast in the mess hall one morning, Cronen told us that tomorrow we were going out to CAP III. I wondered how he knew that. I was learning that some guys were briefed by the brass or the higher-up muckety-mucks and then information was passed by word of mouth down to us grunts. Seemed I'd always be the last to know what the hell was going on. But what did I care? No big deal. I was just along for the ride.

"What's a CAP III?" I asked.

"CAP stands for Combined Action Program and is designed to combine one squad of up to thirteen marines and a corpsman with a fifteen- to twenty-man platoon of local forces in order to defend a village, or possibly several villages, in a TAOR (tactical area of responsibility). Sometimes there will be a full platoon of marines and a company of local forces. It's a means of extending the forces available by using the local PF [Popular Forces]. A PF is a group of locals equivalent to the National Guard in the US but not trained as well and having much worse equipment. The locals in the group are usually older youth and elderly men from the nearby theoretically pacified village.

I learned that Combined Action Platoons are frequently semi-isolated and independent units located near the village(s) they are assigned to protect.

So our squad was going to live in or near a local village that was theoretically in favor of our occupation and war against Ho Chi Min and the Communists while sharing counterinsurgency duties with people who could very well be VC (Vietcong) guerrillas themselves. I didn't like that idea.

The next day, a few trucks showed up and the entire Third Platoon was loaded for transport to CAP III. I was happy about that, as I had at first thought it would be only Cronen's squad. So we had approximately thirty to forty of us going out there—maybe a few more than that.

When we got there, we found a few huts for the Vietnamese and a few sandbag hooches for the marines. It was located in the thick of the forest, surrounded by some barbed wire fencing enclosing the camp. Large open fields around us were filled with large bushes, plants with long leaves, and tall grasses, making it ideal for concealing a stealth attack on us. Thick jungle surrounded us after that. The road in and out was the only break in our forest-walled enclosure. There was no sign of a village.

I looked around and felt completely vulnerable. The barbed wire fencing gave me no sense of security, and the Vietnamese PF guys I saw looked as if they'd run at the first sight of incoming. I wasn't sure that they were not VC in disguise.

We found a hooch, and there were cots available, plus a number of ammo boxes that made up our table and chairs. It was dark and dank inside, but it was a roof against the rain. I shared it with Cronen, Heath, Limmer, Dasher, Blacky, and Smitty.

After we settled in, I got Heath to snap a picture of us "trippin'" on a candle while listening to music on Smitty's boom box. We were trippin' on "Soul Man," by Sam and Dave (my personal favorite); "Sitting on the Dock of the Bay," by Otis Redding; "We Gotta Get out of This Place," by the Animals; and so many other great songs from the era.

Over the next two or three months, Limmer and Dasher would be killed. Cronen and Smitty would be wounded. Heath, Blacky, and I would skate through unscathed. To me, that seems to have been about the average percentage of casualties for grunts in the bush. It was about 30 percent killed, 30 percent wounded, and 40 percent being lucky. Happenstance decides what happens to whom.

We were assigned perimeter positions for night watch and in case of attack. After becoming familiar with our perimeter holes and the path to them, the next thing to do was clean the weapons and get prepared. I spent at least an hour cleaning the M16 and organizing magazines and my 3.5-inch rocket launcher. I was the new "Rockets" guy, and we were currently still using the super bazooka instead of the lighter, more flexible LAAWS (light antitank assault weapons), which were simply shoulder-launched rocket-propelled grenades.

After finishing cleanup and preparation, I took my boots and socks off and reclined in my cot, nothing else going on. Almost immediately, we received a volley of incoming small arms fire. Shit! I grabbed the M16 and ran barefoot out to my hole at the perimeter. On the way, I stepped on something that hurt my bare foot, which gave way and twisted my ankle. Down I went into the muddy trail leading to my perimeter hole.

My nice clean M16 dove barrel first into the mud in an attempt to keep me upright but failed miserably. I scrambled to my knees and crawled the rest of the way, staying low below the incoming rounds. I could tell they were close because the rounds were still cracking and popping as they whizzed past our heads. I was told that the loud, sharp "cracks" were caused by mini sonic booms as they flew past our ears faster than the speed of sound.

Most of the platoon returned fire, and the firefight soon ended. The short duration made it seem to have been the local VC welcoming Kilo to the area, promising another party soon.

I didn't return fire, as my M16 was now plugged with mud. At least my boots and socks didn't get wet or muddy, but now I needed to clean my weapon once again. I was not pleased.

Based on the attack that day and intelligence received from the battalion area, our lieutenant decided to pull a trick on the enemy. We expected a ground attack on the compound sometime that night. The lieutenant thought it was a good idea if after dark we sneaked out of the compound and set up an ambush in the tree line; when they mounted their attack, we would surprise them from the rear.

After dark, the entire platoon slipped into the darkness and out to the tree line. We spread out along it and settled in. Then I heard someone whisper, "Basteen, up."

Huh?

"Basteen, the lieutenant wants to see you at the CP."

Aw, shit. Now what?

I got up and made my way to Lieutenant Ruggles, who was Third Platoon commander. He was standing in the dark under a banana or palm tree with a large black guy, I think named Hinton. The lieutenant looked at me and said, "You are going out with Private Hinton, and you'll be our listening post. If you see or hear anything, come back here and report to me."

"Sir, yes, sir," I said, as if I were back in boot camp, except I whispered it instead of yelling it. That was the first time the lieutenant had spoken to me. I didn't think he even knew I was there, let alone knew my name.

Hinton started out slogging across the rice paddy, which had water in it about up to our ankles. I wondered why we didn't walk along the tree line to the other side, staying in the dark. But no, we headed straight across, splashing with every step. There was a moon out, and I'm sure we were lit up like a Christmas tree. I was new here, but this didn't seem the correct way of doing things. At least, I didn't like it one bit.

As we approached the other side, Hinton stopped and asked me, "Did you hear that?"

I replied, "No, I didn't hear anything except us splashing in the rice paddy."

He continued toward the tree line. I followed. When he got within ten to twenty feet of it, he stopped again and asked, "Did you hear that?"

I replied, "No, I didn't hear anything except us splashing the rice paddy."

Hinton said, "I'm getting out of here." He turned and started route-stepping as fast as he could in the ankle-deep mud of the rice paddy, back to the platoon and the lieutenant. I decided that I was not staying out there alone, so I turned and splashed my way back too.

Back at the CP, Hinton had already told the lieutenant that he heard something in the tree line. I arrived and the lieutenant asked me if I heard anything. I replied, "No, I didn't hear anything."

The lieutenant seemed a little indecisive about what to do next. He decided to send us out there again and be the listening post. Therefore, off we went, Hinton in the lead, once again slogging across the moon-illuminated rice paddy. I was not happy about all this slogging out in the open, especially if Hinton had actually heard something. I was worried and anxious. If there was actually someone there, they knew exactly where we were and where we came from. We were sitting ducks and so was the entire platoon.

No matter. When we get fairly close to the tree line, Hinton thought he heard something and we ended up returning to the lieutenant exactly as before. Back at the CP, Hinton had already told the lieutenant that he heard something in the tree line. When I arrived, the lieutenant asked me if I heard anything. I replied, "No, I didn't hear anything." This time, the lieutenant said to stay in and take our positions. We did.

Nothing happened for the rest of the night, I'm sure because our idiotic splashing across the rice paddy in a nearly full moon ruined our element of surprise. They would have been deaf, dumb, and blind not to determine what was going on. I think the lieutenant realized we had blown it also because we stayed in the following nights.

From then on, we ran day patrols from our CAP III location and got feet soaked crossing small streams every day. Socks were always wet, never dry. Clothes were muddy, dirty, and sweaty. There were no showers or mess hall.

On one day patrol, Louisiana was point and triggered a hand grenade booby trap in a dense clump of trees about a half mile from the village we were protecting. It messed up his legs pretty well, but he accepted the pain and never yelled, screamed, or even complained. That was one tough marine. I hoped I was that tough when my time came, which I was quite sure would come eventually. We cut down two small bamboo trees and used a poncho to make a stretcher. We had to carry him to an open area where the helicopter could land and medevac him out.

Going through the ville, helping carry the makeshift stretcher with Louisiana aboard, I accidentally stepped on a clay pot, which I broke, by one of the family hooches. I wanted to apologize to the mama-san, who I could see was distraught at the loss, but we kept moving. We finally got him to a clearing and choppered him out. I wouldn't see him again.

★★★

Marble Mountain is about five miles south of Da Nang International Airport and reaches almost to the sea. It is actually several large hills grouped together that seem to form a tall island tower overlooking the flat surrounding rice paddies and jungled terrain, located close to the sea. It stands alone and has a most distinctive look. It is a Vietnamese holy area. There was an army base there that may have included special forces operations (Green Berets), prisoners of war, and some other government operations groups, but it was not a typical infantry base.

One night while we were at CAP III, they were attacked by a strong and well-coordinated surprise attack that included sappers getting into the base and NVA, probably helped by VC within the base and disguised as villagers working in their kitchens. In three hours or so of all-out fighting, the base was nearly overrun. The attacking force was finally defeated.

The next day, we hiked over there to secure the area and help with cleanup. I remember walking through the base and seeing the lookout tower burned and broken. The rest of the area was a mess, with every building showing battle damage. The remnants of war littered the grounds. As we walked through the area, all I could think was that it had to have been a night of terror for these guys. I had only been there less than three weeks, and this was the worst battle damage I'd yet seen. I was shocked and scared that this could actually happen. An entire base was nearly overrun, and several people were killed or wounded. This was a real wake-up call for me to the reality of this war. It could be brutal.

Back at CAP III, it was suddenly December 24, 1967. We got the word that trucks would pick us up and return us to the battalion area. We arrived back to the base in the late afternoon to a street lined with tables of beer on ice and steaks cooking on the barbie! After dropping gear on our cots, we lined up. First was the beer line, where we guzzled beer while standing in line waiting for the steaks to heat somewhat past the "moo" stage. Then we did it again. It was a round-robin of gorging ourselves, drinking ourselves sick, and then heading on down the line to the temporary stage set up for the all-female Korean rock band.

I can't remember if the songs were in English or Korean. I didn't even care. The music was great; the steaks were great. The beers were great and seemingly endless. It wasn't raining. Life was good.

Then, suddenly, *kaboom!* We received incoming mortars. Everyone scattered. I ran and jumped into a trench built just for such occasions. It was about three feet across and about three feet deep. There were trenches like this scattered around in most of the areas around the battalion area.

I waited to see if it was safe to get out. I heard our return mortars and some artillery rounds outbound. Nobody else was leaving the trench, so I just stayed there. There were other people on duty tonight, and I was in no condition to be firing a weapon anyway.

When I awoke in the morning, I found I had been sleeping in a stream of mud running down the trench. It had rained sometime last night, although I never knew it. I probably looked like shit; I know that the guy I woke up next to sure did. His eyes were blurry red, he had a growth of beard, his hair was matted down and muddy, and his clothes were dirty, splotchy, muddy pieces of green cloth. His soft cover was half drowned in the stream of mud.

I laughed and said, "Ha, morning, sunshine."

He said, "Yeah, sure shit."

I didn't know this guy, but obviously he was from Kilo 3/5, so I asked, "Who are you and who are you with?"

He answered, "Ron McCarville, Second Platoon."

I said, "Bruce Bastien, weapons platoon, but everybody calls me Basteen."

He replied, "Good to know. See ya later." We climbed out of the trench. I noticed Cronen crawling out of the trench a little farther down the way. He didn't look any better than the rest of us.

It became December 31, 1967, and Cronen's squad got the night patrol. We left just after sunset and dark. We wandered a long ways for a long time and then set up another ambush near a road. I didn't realize that this was New Year's Eve until midnight, when we saw the fireworks. Every place with US military personnel seemed to have weapons firing into the air at the same time. We saw fireworks from three or four different places, spread all around the area, go up at the same time. It was probably midnight! (Duh.) *That sure was a waste of ammo*, I thought derisively.

Finally, we headed back and got back in the battalion area just about first light in the morning. I was still wired and awake from the patrol, so when I get to my cot, I turned on my radio. To my great surprise, I was listening live to the Green Bay Packers and Dallas NFL Championship football game. Did I hear that right? It was thirteen degrees below zero. They were playing at Lambeau Field, an outdoor open-air stadium in Green Bay, Wisconsin, and the game would come to be called the "Ice Bowl."

Being from Minneapolis and experiencing those brutal winters, I laughed when I heard it. I certainly wasn't missing Minnesota then. Suddenly, I thought maybe I didn't have it so bad here after all. Here I was in the tropics, having a nice warm winter, while they were all trying to convince themselves that they were tough and having fun tailgating in thirteen degrees below zero weather. Given enough alcoholic antifreeze in your system, you can convince yourself of anything, I guess.

McShane, Wilson, Farmer, and English at the An Hoa Combat Base. I show this here because I did not have a camera yet at this time and didn't have pictures of the original 3/5 Battalion area, but most bases looked and functioned somewhat similarly.

Smitty, (I have forgotten who was next), Hawthorne, and Waterman back in An Hoa

Terry Waterman on some patrol late in the year, but this is what it looked like to me on my first day patrol back out of the Battalion area.

Wilson and me on one of our daily patrols in December 1967, out of the Battalion area. We were always getting our feet wet.

This is later in the year, somewhere on some operation, but it is representative of our daily patrols out of the Battalion area back in December of 1967.

This is at CAP III. Heath was taking the picture, and from left to right are Cronen, Limmer, Smitty, Blacky, Dasher, and Bastien. Within a few months, Limmer and Dasher would be dead; Cronen and Smitty would be wounded; and Blacky, Heath, and I would escape unharmed.

CHAPTER 8

ANDERSON BRIDGE

Shortly after the New Year's Eve "Ice Bowl," we were booted out of the battalion area. Maybe they were still mad at us for not cleaning up the mess after the Christmas Eve party. No matter … They dispersed us to different locations, and we were spread out pretty thin. Third Platoon went to Anderson Bridge for patrols and bridge duty.

Anderson Bridge was somewhere near the 3/5 Battalion area and crossed a good-sized river that flowed to the sea. I think the road that crossed it passed the Battalion area on the way into Da Nang. The river flowed west to east. The road went north and south. I was assigned the northwest quadrant with Cronen, Brown, Maddy, Daisher, Aycock, and some others whose names I can no longer remember. Lieutenant Ruggles was in command at the bridge. Lieutenant Ruggles was Kilo 3 actual. He was a little taller than most, only a little older than most, and wore big round glasses larger than my Marine Corps–issue glasses. It made him look wiser and more authoritative than we did. Otherwise, he dressed like us and looked like us, but we somehow could sense that we took orders from him.

On the south side of the river, about a quarter mile down the road, was a village to the southeast quadrant along with a US Army compound and artillery battery to the southwest side of the road. They had a mess hall, and simply for contributing a few marines to help with mess duty, we were able to eat hot, real chow. Our days at the bridge were filled with day patrols or bridge duty, and the nights were filled with night patrols or bridge duty. Squads rotated through the different duties. By most standards, this was good duty. It was middle to late January 1968.

Rick Maddy took his turn at the various different duties like the rest of us. He told me a story about finding himself on nighttime bridge watch with Private First Class Aycock. They were on duty watching the river flow past, looking for debris in the river that could be carrying explosives timed to go off at the bridge. They had a box full of new grenades just for blowing up any suspicious debris coming downstream.

They realized that they had another long night and several boring hours of idle time ahead of them. After throwing a few grenades out into the river to eliminate suspicious objects, Maddy had a great idea! He would instead drop the grenades straight down into the water by the bridge pilings. The grenade sunk well below and exploded underwater. The bridge shook like an earthquake had hit it, and a fountain of bubbling water boiled to the top. In Maddy's words, "This is cool."

To add to his fun, Maddy decided to pull the pin. He let the spoon fly, counted to three, and then tossed it down. This allowed the grenade to sink only a little below the river top, and when it exploded, it resulted in a brilliant white flash and more water thrown up into the air. Maddy said, "This is even more cool."

Sometime after midnight in the pitch-black night, a bug-eyed Maddy pulled the pin, let the spoon fly, counted to three, and dropped the grenade. *Kaboom!* The grenade went off *above* the waterline. White and red pieces of shrapnel flew everywhere. The bridge was peppered with fragments.

A marine on shore screamed, "Incoming!"

Marines streamed out of their hooches and headed for their fighting holes. I was one of those marines wondering what was happening. Were they mortars? Where they through the wire? Maddy couldn't see a thing except the huge white spot right in front of his eyes, but he yelled, "No incoming," and he concealed his foolishness by yelling, "Short fuse on the grenade!"

Things settled down. Maddy was embarrassed for waking everybody and for doing something that could have caused a casualty. The rest of us returned to doing what we were doing. No big deal—just another night at Anderson Bridge.

I took my turn at different duties and day and night patrol as well. I also took my turn sitting out near the wire on listening watch at night. That was *not* good duty. The hole out there was a one-person hole for listening and watching to ensure no ground attack happened, at least without warning, for the people on the bridge. It was manned continually throughout the night. It was located thirty or forty yards from the bridge on the path that led to the barbed wire perimeter fence and the tree line beyond that. It was a lonely, scary outpost, seemingly miles from any help. I felt alone. I was alone. Every time I come out there, I was scared shitless.

The path to the hole was a narrow dirt path with chest-high vegetation all the way to the barbed wire fence and to the tree line, which was another fifty yards beyond that.

I stood in the hole, which was about three feet deep. Or sometimes I sat on the edge staring outward down the trail into the darkness. The tree line beyond was completely black. Just past the hole, there was a small rise in the trail leading to the perimeter. Standing in the hole or sitting on the edge made it impossible to see over the vegetation or past the rise in the trail. I determined that I would not be standing outside the hole. I wouldn't be seeing anything, but if I heard something, I would be throwing grenades.

At night, there simply was no light unless we had a moon. I could barely see my hands in front of my face. The army compound on the other side of the river and a quarter mile down the road did provide some light, but only a faint glow. Where I was, it was completely still and black. It was a spooky and lonely quiet.

I listened for any sounds. My eyes played tricks on my brain. My ears were conspiring with my eyes. I saw movement that wasn't there. I heard noises that really didn't happen. I was afraid to breathe. I was wound tight. I waited and was expecting somebody to walk or crouch over that small rise in front of me at any time. My M16 was loaded, safety off, on full automatic, and pointed. Grenades were laid out and handy. I waited and watched nervously, expecting gooks in from the wire. I was sure I heard the wire being cut.

After a long two hours, somebody walked up from the bridge to replace me. It was now somebody else's turn. I headed back to my cot, stomach in knots and worn out from two hours of tension. Waiting for shit to happen was the worst thing of all. Waiting with anticipation and expectation built anxiety that built imagination, which built nervous tension. I got to the cot, but I'd not sleep until I wound down from the adrenaline high of a nighttime at listening watch, alone in the dark.

It was now late January or early February of 1968. We were still at Anderson Bridge. It got to be sunset, and Lieutenant Ruggles told Steve Cronen that he and his squad would be going out on patrol that night. Cronen would be squad leader. He also got to walk point. It would be Steve, Brown, two others, and me.

We set off from the road through the jungle for the river and the start of our patrol. We followed the river for a long while and then turned away inland. We walked for a long time. We skirted the rice paddies, penetrated the jungle, crossed roads and paths, and we stayed in the dark areas and passed through a village or two. I followed (as tail-end Charlie once again) and wondered how Steve could possibly know where he was going. It was so dark that I could barely see the guy in front of me, but I would not fall behind. I would not get separated.

Finally, we started back. It had been a quiet and uneventful patrol. As long as we were moving, the mosquitoes didn't bother us. It was a warm and muggy evening. We were sweating even though it had not been a particularly difficult walk.

We were crossing a big field of very tall elephant grass about a click away (one thousand meters) from the bridge. We saw and heard a helicopter heading our way. It was one of those with the big bright searchlights on them. He was sweeping the area and lighting up everything under that big light, looking for the bad guys. He found us and got us in his light. It was bright as day, and we are highlighted. I imagined we were in his sights as well. I expected him to open up on us at any moment. Cronen popped a green flare, signifying that we were the good guys.

The problem was that three green flares went up into the night sky! Ours was in the middle. We were exactly between the other two green flares, and neither was very far away.

The chopper was satisfied and left the area. That left us sitting between two other groups; we didn't know who. A radio call to the CP confirmed that there were no "friendlies" in the area. Shit! We sat quietly, trying to decide what to do. I heard talking, and it wasn't English. They had to know we were here. There seemed to be several on each side of us. What were they going to do about us? They weren't doing anything. Could it be that they didn't know we were here? How could that possibly be? What was going on?

Cronen decided that we should get out of there and get back to the bridge, and because they let us, that was exactly what we did. We route-stepped, walking as fast as we possibly could through the field all the way back to the bridge. We weren't worried about being stealthy.

Back at the bridge, the lieutenant was trying to get us to "go back out there and find out who that is" when the rockets started inbound. The incredibly loud, scary screech of an incoming rocket would scare the shit out of you. It got louder the closer it got, and it moved very fast. It sounded like, and I pictured, the Grim Reaper shrieking in on a burning bull to drag us off to hell.

The rockets got one of the tanks right off but never did get the second. There were mortar rounds, rockets, and small arms coming in. We hit the deck next to our hooch. The lieutenant ran off to his command post. I was watching the trail out to the listening post hole, but I was not going out there.

The attack ended later, when the healthy tank crossed the bridge and began firing into the tree line. They were never able to disable both tanks. The firepower of a tank is awesome. It would cut down jungle trees. I saw some trees fall that night. A tank round, I was told, consisted of thousands of small dart-like metal arrows. I was sure that was why a ground attack didn't hit us. They couldn't stand up to that.

I was pretty well convinced that the only reason we got back to the bridge at all was because they were more interested in the rocket attack on the bridge than they were in one small squad of marines in the bush. That was another event that got into my "close calls" scoreboard. The five of us had walked right through their ambush. Then the incoming rockets had missed us standing on the bridge. I wondered again how many narrow escapes I got.

As it turned out, although nobody knew it at the time, this was the beginning of the Tet Offensive—at least for our unit at Anderson Bridge. The incoming rockets had destroyed a shitter and damaged the lookout tower, but nobody was killed. We were all lucky. The guy in the shitter at the time was injured. I received a bloody nose but don't remember how. Once you hear it, the sound of incoming rockets is not something you'll ever forget. It is a terrifying *swoosh-scream* sound that ends in a terrifyingly loud explosion.

Years later, Rick Maddy (of grenades on the bridge fame) would write of this very same event at the bridge from his viewpoint:

> I was sitting on my bunk staring at my boots. I hadn't seen my feet for well over a week. I was scared, and I wasn't going to get caught by the gooks with my pants down or boots off. The other marines that had been in country for much longer were getting naked, bathing, and swimming in the river.
>
> Ballsy stuff! I thought. Not me. FNG-itis.
>
> I still preferred being Private Crud, with my boots on. I made my decision. I had heard the stories, the ones about some guy taking his boots off and leaving half of his jungle-rotted foot inside it. Tonight I was taking off my boots and getting a good night's sleep—a good night's sleep being one with minimal bone-jarring jerks awake. I never was able to "sleep" in Vietnam.
>
> I removed my boots and my socks. I did a double take on my feet. They were green. The green dye of my government-issue Marine Corps green socks, combined with the constant wet, was now the color of my feet.
>
> What the hell!
>
> All of a sudden, something came screeching in. *Boom!*
>
> Tipton jumped off his bunk, grabbed his gear, and yelled at me that it was incoming and headed out the hatch. I couldn't believe this was happening. I hurriedly put on my socks and then my boots. The intensity of incoming was getting greater all the time. I grabbed my rifle and ammo, and out the door I went.
>
> My hole was probably twenty yards away. I was running in a crouched position, and two more screeching rockets made their way in simultaneously—a noise one never forgets. I hit the deck. Boom! Boom! One landed to my left. The ground shook. The shrapnel swooshed by me.
>
> I jumped up and took a few more steps, literally falling into the safety of my hole. I didn't feel hurt or sick. No shock. I couldn't see a damn thing; it was pitch-black. I must be okay. I couldn't believe I wasn't nailed.
>
> My luck was running out. Private First Class Aycock, who was supposed to be with me in this hole, was over at the army artillery unit doing mess duty. The army had been letting us eat chow over there as long as we sent a couple of marines over to help in the mess. Tonight was Aycock's turn. And I was alone, scared shitless, shaking with tremors, and trying to keep my muzzle above my head to keep from shooting myself accidentally.

Another rocket came in and hit near us. S*chhhhhhhh!* The shrapnel passed over my hole. I *was* not going to stick my head out of this hole.

Then I came to my senses. The gooks were going to come across the wire. I had to look. I started peering above the edge of my hole. No small arms fire that I could detect was being fired at us. I saw mortar shells exploding as they tried to walk them into the gun position on my left. They failed to hit it.

On my right, a rocket hit one of the hooches. I would find out later that Private First Class Crockett was in it, buried in sandbags and bleeding from the ears. Someone in the southwest sector on the other side of the road accidentally set off a teargas canister. The prevailing winds were in my favor. Across the river came yelling for whoever was up in the tower to evacuate it.

There were red flashes coming from the tree line at my twelve o'clock, possibly the launch area for the rockets or the flash of a mortar tube. Someone called for the tank to cross the river. I watched as the tank, with about only six inches on each side to spare, slowly made its way across the bridge. I was thinking about the pilings that had taken a hell of a pounding from the grenades I had been dropping next to them. The bridge held, and the tank arrived on the west side.

The army artillery unit was now firing large illumination flares from a very close proximity to our position. The shells popped open, releasing their candlepower, and the casings spiraling toward the ground with their *whoop, whoop, whoop* sound. I now had anxiety about getting beaned by one of those damn things.

Still no gooks in the wire.

The tank commander yelled, "Everybody down; fire in the hole!" I wasn't going to miss this. Zeroing in on where the flashes had been spotted, the tank fired its 90 mm. The tracer round penetrated into the tree line. Boom! The tank kept firing into the tree line. More rockets and mortars landed in our perimeter.

Shells were hitting all around. They didn't seem to be trying to hit the bridge. They must have wanted to keep it intact. Crazy thoughts raced through my head. They couldn't aim those things, could they? They were gooks! They must have been after the tank and us. So where were they?

Still no gooks in the wire.

The tank kept up the fire and then was hit by a rocket. Then silence.

Morning's light came. Charlie decided he didn't want to come inside the compound. Hit, do some damage, and then run. The bridge was intact. The tower still stood tall. Nobody killed or wounded, although I would have considered Private First Class Crockett, with his ears bleeding, as wounded. Pieces of rocket fragments were lying around. We even found a tail section. The tank was hit but not penetrated.

The tank had its large spotlight blown apart. It was a dangling mess. There was a nice dent in the turret where the rocket had hit. Large and small holes had pierced the outside railings on the tank's body. One was almost big enough to put my fist through it. Even today, when I see one of those light beams going into the air from some sale downtown, I think of that tank.

I had survived a night of terror on Anderson Bridge, a place that had started out as good duty. Besides several inbound mortar shells, no fewer than six rockets had landed in the northwest sector—one just before I left my hooch; two hit as I was on my way to my hole; another passed its shrapnel over my hole while I was in it—one that hit Private First Class Daisher's hooch and the one that nailed the tank. I was beginning to get the picture. This was a very serious place. What the rocket shrapnel had done to the tank would cause a person to turn into hamburger. I was never the same after that night.

I cannot recall the next time I removed my boots.

CHAPTER 9

THE OLD FRENCH FORT

The Tet Offensive was now in progress across most of Vietnam. The attack on Anderson Bridge occurred in the first day or so of February 1968, but I could be wrong about that. Most cities and military targets were being attacked, and some were being overrun by the surprise attacks. Of course, we grunts didn't know any of that. For us, it was business as usual, one patrol or watch after another, not knowing when things might change. The attack on the bridge was a surprise but just another something we endured and expected to happen at some point in time.

But we had a feeling something was up when we were told to saddle up—we were being moved again. Of course, we didn't know where. Kilo was to remain split apart, with First Platoon going somewhere. I did not know where (the marine base at Phu Bai, I believe) and Second and Third Platoons going to the old French fort.

We loaded onto the backs of trucks for the haul through Da Nang, past the Seventh Army Motor Pool and up the mountains to the north. I hadn't been here yet. It was all new to me. There was a rugged range of mountains that divided northern South Vietnam from Da Nang and the rest of central South Vietnam to the south. We lumbered up Highway 1 to Hai Van Pass at the top of the divide, where there was an army base. The army base had a supply center and a mess hall, I was told. Naturally, we passed right on by and started down the other side.

Continuing along the winding, narrow two-lane road (not a highway by our standards), we began to get wonderful glimpses of the area known as the "Bowling Alley," so named because the several mountains and peaks to our north appeared somewhat like a bowling alley when viewed from the other end of the long narrow valley that eventually spread out to our northwest.

The view from our open-air tourist vehicles was impressive but a little scary, as we were on the cliffside of the road. The drop-off down the mountain was long and steep, and in some places, there was not more than a foot from road to cliff. The mountains were steep and rugged, thick with rain forests. Way down below were the remnants of a railroad that wound its way from Hue City to Da Nang by circumnavigating around the mountains and staying along the coast. The South China Sea, shimmering and shining in the midday sun, lay only a few horizontal miles out from our mountain road, but it was a long way down.

We traveled a few miles down from Hai Van Pass, following the crest of these mountains and on somewhat of a slight downgrade. We arrived at our new temporary home. Turning left, our trucks struggled to climb a short, steep uphill dirt road to an open plateau. The plateau seemed to have been chopped out of the mountainside. It was about fifty feet above Highway 1 and was marked by the same steep drop-off at the edge down to the highway as we had on our drop-off side of the road down to the sea below.

Back from the drop-off, nestled in a big, open clearing, rested the old French fort, with steep mountains rising just behind as a backdrop. Where the clearing ended, we were surrounded by a rain forest. Behind the castle-like fortification was a good-sized stream flowing down from the mountains and forest above, and a small waterfall dropped into a canyon that carried the stream past our new temporary home and then farther downhill.

The old French fort had obviously been here since the French occupation. It appeared solid and secure, surrounded by tall stone and cement walls and a main gate that could allow our trucks into the compound, if desired. My impression was that it was similar to the old, massive fortifications in France and throughout Europe, North Africa, and the Middle East. We unloaded from the trucks, and as I viewed the new surroundings, I was thinking that this looked good—safe, secure—and I was picturing cots in a hooch inside the walls, plus probably a mess hall and showers. It was a picturesque location and view. I might like to vacation there some day when the fort became a hotel.

As it turned out, I never saw the inside of those walls. There were no mess halls or showers. We pitched ponchos into our two-man pup tents with sticks just as if we were on operation—outside the fortress walls. We got a resupply of four C rations meals. We *were* on operation, and this was our new command post. We would be running day and night ops from there for a while. There were a few sandbagged hooches located around the outside, but they seemed already occupied.

Collocated with us was an ARVN (Army of the Republic of Vietnam) company. They didn't seem friendly or appreciative of us, and relations were tense. They had some tents on the other side of the fort, near the end of the clearing.

We settled in and found fighting holes in case of attack. There was nothing else to do tonight, so I linked up with Hawthorne, MGM (Marvin Gerald Monroe), and Harmon for a game of hearts or poker; I can't remember which. Harmon had commandeered one of the sandbagged hooches on the edge of the drop off to Highway 1. It was a good decision, as it afforded him and his M60 machine gun a good view and coverage of the road up to the plateau.

We noticed that there were some large rats around the fort. We saw them running along the tops of the cement walls surrounding the stronghold. We saw some running in the vegetation just outside Harmon's hooch. Harmon was disturbed by this and went somewhere to retrieve a large rattrap. Large rattraps were in supply here. They were aware of the problem.

Harmon showed us this monster rattrap. It was a standard mousetrap on steroids. It looked strong enough to break fingers if one got careless. That was good because these rats, from what I saw, were big, mean, and nasty beasties. Harmon opened a can of C ration sliced ham salted in preservatives and put a hunk in the trap. He gingerly set the trap and slid it down the slope several inches. We restarted our card game.

Whap! The trap snapped shut. We were all impressed that we got one so quickly. Harmon grabbed the trap, grabbed the rat (a big one), and tossed it downhill. So we waited while he reset and rebaited the trap. He slid it a few inches down the hill, and we restarted the card game.

Whap! The trap snapped shut. We were all impressed that we had gotten another one so quickly. Harmon grabbed the trap, grabbed the rat (another big one), and tossed it downhill. So we waited again while he reset and rebaited the trap. He slid it a few inches down the hill, and we restarted the card game.

Whap! The trap snapped shut. Now we were all pissed because these damn rats were interfering with our game. This time Harmon grabbed the trap and the rat and tossed both downhill. We decided there were too many rats and to just let them be. We wouldn't reset the trap again.

★★★

We started running operations out of the old French fort. Some were up the hill, into the mountains. Some were down the hill, into the valley, jungle, and streams. Corporal Ron Heath recounted the next incident. He later became our unofficial company historian. Ron Heath had been with us since our CAP III days. He had become a squad leader in the weapons platoon and was with us now. He wrote the following:

> It was February 1968. We hadn't been at the French fort for more than a few days. The weather was a fine misting rain that was barely distinguishable from fog except that you got wet faster. Water beaded up on the leaves and tended to soak you as you brushed against them. You didn't have to travel far to be soaked to the skin. The solution: rain gear. My parents had sent me a heavy-duty set from home, and they worked great. The rain pants were like a farmer's bib overalls, and the jacket was a rubberized pullover type, like a sweatshirt with a hood. No way was I going to get wet unless it was from sweat.
>
> This was our first patrol of the Bowling Alley area since arriving at the French fort. Lieutenant Ruggles decided that we would be patrolling about a half klick down from the highway, with a shielding of brush to give us concealment. There were no trails. The ground was firm but spongy and gave good traction. The point man was moving at a comfortably brisk pace. We had moved through the underbrush and crossed some streams for about an hour or so when the lieutenant called a halt, set out the watch, and we took a break. We were hot and sweaty from the pace of the patrol, and we started taking off our rain jackets. Then came the discovery. One of the men had a leech on him. Lieutenant Ruggles passed the word around to check for leeches. I found mine right away. It was on my left forearm, still wiggling around and looking for a place to settle in and feed. I got him right away with my Zippo.
>
> I wasn't a smoker, but I carried a lighter out of habit. You never knew when you needed to light a fire.
>
> Off came shirts, and up came trouser legs to check for the dreaded creatures. Trousers were dropped and inspections made. There were leeches on shins, covering backs and posteriors, and were on various parts of arms and legs. The lighters came out, the cigarettes were fired up, and everyone began to burn leeches. Then came the howl. One of the men had found a leech on his pecker. Well, not really on his pecker; he had gone to take a leak and found himself stoppered by a swollen leech. It was inside his pecker, with the tail of the leech hanging partway out. His cry for help hadn't gone unanswered. The first helpful volunteer had flipped open his Zippo and fired it up. Now the protest wasn't about the leeches but the damage the flame of the Zippo would do to the tip of the very sensitive equipment. A compromise was made, and the Zippo was used to light up a cigarette. The leech was coaxed out with the burning end of the cigarette gingerly applied to the affected area. It was a bloody mess. I had never realized just how big leeches could become in such a short feeding time.

I thanked my parents many times during the monsoon season for my rainsuit. I always kept my rain pants bloused at the boots, and that kept me from having any leeches on the bottom half of my body.

★★★

We continued our stay at the French fort with a series of day patrols and night ambushes. A typical night ambush consisted of two marines going out with two ARVN. The patrol would sneak out just after dark and very stealthily find a spot that was a likely approach avenue for the VC or NVA to get to the fort and attack it. Then the patrol would hide in the vegetation and take turns sleeping or watching until the bad guys approached and we'd take them out. That was the idea.

My turn came one night, when I was paired with another grunt from Third Platoon. It may have been "Blacky" Blackwelder, Don Mobeck, or any one of several others. I don't remember.

It was twilight, and we met our two ARVN at the gate. I think it was Mobeck who led the group. I was following him, and the two ARVN were in tow. We paralleled Highway 1 for a short while and then headed uphill, up the mountain, and then we backtracked toward the old French fort. Finally, we settled in within shooting distance of the fort and up behind it. (After all, the idea was to protect it from attack.) The four of us settled into a good cover and waited.

Then in the darkness, the stillness, and the quiet of the early night, the ARVNs started talking out loud. I couldn't believe it. I tried to shush them, but they looked at me as if I was crazy and just kept chattering away as if they were at the market or something. I couldn't shut them up. I should have shot them, but that would have given away our position. I couldn't do anything about it. I thought they were trying to alert the VC that we were there. Or maybe they were frightened and wanted to keep the VC away by making noise.

Mobeck and I did not think this was a good idea, so we upped and moved. We moved over to the other side of the stream that ran down to the fort and made a waterfall. We set up in there and found good cover. We also had a great view down the mountain, right out to the South China Sea. The only bad thing was that we each had two or three two-hour watches ahead of us this night.

It was midnight when I started my turn. Mobeck was in the fetal position on the ground, lying on some green stuff and under some bushes. It started raining. It continued to rain, not a downpour rain but a continuous soft, steady rain, perfect for the garden. It soaked everything. All my clothes were washing machine wet, including my soft cover, shirt, utilities, boots, and weapon. My glasses were blurry with raindrops, a river of water dropped off my nose like the waterfall we were watching, and water dribbled down my back inside my shirt. It was cold water.

It was finally 2:00 a.m., and I woke Mobeck, although he wasn't really sleeping. He knew it was his turn at watching the rainfall. He sat up. I didn't want to lie down in the mud, so I sat holding my knees up to my chest. Miraculously, just as we switched roles, the rain stopped. I was thinking, *Wow, we should have done this earlier.* Unfortunately, just after the rain stopped, the wind picked up. It was a strong wind off the ocean just out in front of us. We were high up the mountain, and it was already chilly to begin with.

The wind blew for the rest of the night. By the time it was my watch again, I was shivering so much that I couldn't have picked up my rifle if the bad guys had come along and announced their arrival. My teeth were chattering so loudly that anybody could have heard it for fifty yards. No wonder nobody came by. I couldn't stop the chattering or the shivering. I don't remember ever shivering so much in a Minnesota winter.

We both sat there side by side for the rest of the night, shivering and chattering. At first light, Mobeck suggested that we head back to the fort. We walked way down and around, found Highway 1, and then approached the fort from the access road so the marines on watch there could see who it was and not blow us away inadvertently, thinking we were inbound VC.

As we headed to our poncho homes, Mobeck said, "Hey, you wanna get high?"

I said, "Naw, it never works for me."

Mobeck said, "Come on, try it one more time."

"Okay."

So we headed over to the back side of the fort and sat, still wet and shivering. Mobeck lit up, took a hit, and handed it to me. I inhaled, held my breath as long as I could, and handed it back. We did this a time or two. I soon realized that I was no longer shivering or cold. In fact, as the sun came up and lit up the mountain behind us and the waterfall became blue again, I said, "Wow, what a beautiful day!"

Mobeck laughed.

★★★

On one of the several day or weeklong patrols we took out of the old French fort, we wandered into the rugged coastal mountains north of Hai Van Pass and just along the coast. We were now between Highway 1 and the beaches below, but the terrain was steep and rugged. The jungle was thick and lush rain forest, and it was full of nasty insects and reptiles. The hills were steep and slippery. The vegetation was always wet and full of creepy-crawly critters.

We were on a sweep from one end of this area to the other for several days. It rained most of the time. We were usually wet, cold, and hungry. During the nights, we generally slept alone single file along the trail in ponchos backed up against trees, or curled up in a patch of tall grass, or right there on the trail on the bumpy roots of trees. In the mornings, we usually found a torrent of water running downhill through our ponchos. We were always wet. I was still hoping for immersion foot so I could get medevacked, but that never happened.

Tonight, however, looked to be a good night! The sky was clear, and we were stopping early. Unbelievably, we were still dry. Even better, we had been resupplied today. We had food. The mood was good! Spirits were high. I found myself getting first watch as it became full night. I watched while Mobeck, Wilson, and Hawthorne decided where they wanted to bunk and chow down.

I was uphill somewhat from them somewhat but could still hear them decide to dig a neat bunker where they could eat and sleep in complete comfort and safety. "Yeah, *bueno*," said Hawthorne, our Texan/Mexican Hispanic. I listened as three E-tools chopped away feverishly at the soft ground.

After a while, they had a large deep hole big enough to hold three marines. Ponchos spread across the top and anchored at the sides by mud and rocks formed a roof. They were extremely proud of themselves as they slipped under the ponchos to enjoy a warm, dry meal in secluded safety.

I must admit that they did a good job too because even though I was only a few feet from them, I could just barely see a dim glow through the ponchos from their candle. I could just barely hear whispering. They were congratulating themselves, patting themselves on the back, for a job so well done!

After their C ration feast of ham and lima beans, beans and franks, or ham sliced in preservatives, the candle went out and they settled in for the night. The night was still and quiet. It hadn't been ten minutes since the candle went out. I began hearing or feeling a commotion. Something seemed to be happening, coming from down in the ground. It got louder. There definitely was a romping and a stomping going on somewhere down under the ground. This had me confused! What was this? Where was it coming from? It seemed as it was coming from down in the ground.

I was getting really concerned when suddenly the ponchos over the hole-in-the-ground fortress exploded upward and fell downhill into the wet bush. Mobeck, Wilson, and Hawthorne all followed in one mighty leap and stood by their former bunker, looking at one another while furiously wiping and brushing themselves.

One of them said, "What was that?"

Another replied, "I don't know, but it was on me too!"

The other said, "It crawled right across my chest."

I laughed (couldn't help it). I finished watching them sleep alone, wrapped in their damp muddy ponchos, along the trail but *not* in their insect- and reptile-infested hole.

It was after one of these sweeps where we had been in the bush for quite a while. Suddenly, we were back at the old French fort along Highway 1. On the very first day back, we were told that a convoy would be coming down from the army base at Hai Van Pass, bringing hot meals (real food) from the mess hall. I couldn't wait. This would be *real* food, and I was sure it'd be hot. And sure enough, later that day, the convoy arrived and a flatbed truck with some big pots of food stopped right there on Highway 1.

I was one of the first in line. I don't remember what I was expecting, but the terms *hot meal* and *real food* included visions of mess halls with big brown carrying trays; metal plates; metal silverware; and cups for milk, coffee, or water, with food splashed all over it.

When it was my turn, I looked expectantly at the kid who was serving. He was a young kid in the army. He had a big ladle/spoon in order to spoon out the chili (I think it was) onto the plate or bowl, which I didn't have. He looked at me quizzically and asked, "Where's your mess kit?"

"Huh? Mess kit? I don't have no mess kit." I didn't even have my plastic spoon. (I was used to a can opener and a can of food preservatives, sometimes called C rations.)

He said, "I don't have any mess kits."

I panicked as I realized I might not get any real food today. I looked around quickly. I needed something to put my real food on. I spied an old C rations cardboard box lying in the ditch by the road. It was flattened and about the size of a plate. I grabbed it, shook the dirt off, and told him to put the food there. He dropped a big spoonful onto my cardboard box, and I shoveled the food into my mouth with my fingers. It was red, it was brown, and it was hot ... It was real.

So off they went, but I heard that they would be back tomorrow. Surely they would know that we didn't have mess kits and they would bring some then. Knowing that, I tossed my cardboard box.

Tomorrow came, and just like clockwork, they showed up again. I lined up, and when it was my turn, the same kid said, "Where's your mess kit?"

"Huh? Mess kit? I don't have no mess kit." I didn't even have my plastic spoon.

I now realized and remembered that this was the Marine Corps, and of course they wouldn't bring any mess kits. I panicked again and hurriedly looked around for something to use. Right there on the ground, where I threw it yesterday, was my C rations box from the day before. I picked it up, shook the dirt off, and said, "Put the food here." He gave me a shovelful of chili (I think it was), and I scooped it into my mouth with my fingers.

I finally got smart (sometimes it takes a while). I looked around and noticed that the other marines were using their canteen cup holders as their mess kits. Inside the canteen pouch that we attached to the utility belt was sometimes a metal canteen holder. You placed your metal canteen into the canteen holder. If you needed a mess kit, you pulled out the metal canteen holder from the pouch. It had a foldable handle that could be used to heat the contents over a fire or over a heat tab. It was seldom used that way, however, because it was much easier to simply heat a C rations canned meal over a heat tab. I even had a canteen holder all the time! They don't come any dumber than me, but you live and learn—even a Marine Corps grunt from Minneapolis. After months in the bush, I was at least learning some survival techniques, catching on slowly but surely.

Bastien in the mortar pit behind the old French fort. Hard to see but behind the green vegetation was a sharp drop off to the mountain stream below. It was fed by the waterfall over that ledge of rocks directly behind me, which was actually quite a ways away, and the waterfall was very difficult to see in this picture. The hill goes up quite steeply and was heavily forested from there.

Haycraft at the edge of the cliff overlooking Highway 1 at the old French fort. It was difficult to realize the scale, but if you looked way down the hill toward the ocean, you could just barely see a train bridge over a stream and the train track leading around the mountain. It was far down and far away.

MGM, Larry Hawthorne, and Bastien peeking around from behind the Second Platoon machine gunner Harmon

We were playing cards when Harmon got the rattrap and set it just down the hill. We killed so many rats that we couldn't play cards, so we stopped setting the trap.

Doc McKillip, two ARVN fighters, and Bastien at the old French fort. There were some sandbag hooches and our poncho tents outside the walls. These guys seemed friendly enough, but there was bad blood between ARVN and marines.

H. E. Bakken and other marines getting hot real food at the army "lunch" wagon sent to us two times on Highway 1, just down from the old French fort

There was a huge pail (pot) of hot chow (chili, I think it was) available, but you needed a mess kit or something to hold it. My utensils became an old C ration cardboard box and my fingers.

Second Platoon machine gunner Harmon sitting at his hooch overlooking the approach to the old French fort. He was right at the edge of the cliff and had a good view of the approach to the fort.

CHAPTER 10

MOUNTAIN OPERATIONS

While we were at the old French fort, some of us were deployed to Hai Van Pass with the army base. Some of us weren't. Corporal Heath was a short-timer who was so deployed. Apparently, he had some fun wasting taxpayer dollars and showing off! The following is by Ron Heath from one of our website articles:

Toward the end of my tour, I was getting short and spent most of my time at our company CP. The CP was at Hai Van Pass at the time, and we were cruising. Tet was over, things were fairly quiet, and Third Platoon was perimeter security. We were getting new replacements in fairly regularly now. We had a new skipper. Lieutenant Smith had finished his tour and was rotating to another assignment.

I was running an M60 section and was acting as the squad leader for Third Platoon's gun squad. Rather than carrying my rifle around, I would be gunner for a day and carry a .45-caliber pistol. This particular day, I was doing something to kill time near the landing zone (LZ), which was just up the hill a little from our tent. There was a makeshift firing range in a gully just on the other side of the LZ.

One of the new men, who had just arrived in the country within the past few days, came up to me and asked if I knew how to use the .45 I was carrying. Without saying a word, I popped the flap of my holster open and in one motion drew the pistol, flipped the safety off, pulled the slide back, jacked a round into the chamber, and raised the pistol up to point at a telegraph pole near the LZ. I gave the trigger a squeeze, felt the pistol recoil, and watched the insulator on one of the arms of the telegraph pole disappear in an explosion of glass shards.

I cleared the pistol, put the safety on, and put it back into my holster. I then looked deadpan at the man and said in a low, slow voice straight out of the Old West, "Yep, I guess I do."

His eyes were still wide, and his jaw was only a few inches above the ground as I walked by him to the tent. When I got inside, I had the biggest grin on my face. I don't think I could have repeated that performance in a million years. I was a lousy shot with a .45, but everything felt so right. It was one of those instances where you don't even let your mind think about what you are doing; you just let reflexes take over.

I had this sort of feeling many times during my tour and always let it take over. Believe me, it worked.

★★★

For those of us not so lucky, we still ran operations from the French fort. Many ops were up into the mountains and rain forests along the many trails. Those operations were usually day ops, where I carried my M60 mortar and wore a hard hat but carried no pack. That was like light duty and we were out for a stroll. I don't remember any encounters that ruined the patrol. The entire thing was like a walk in the park, watching and listening to the mountain birds and monkeys. The canopy was beautiful, the skies were blue, the temps were acceptable. It was nice. I would have stayed there for the rest of my tour.

On some patrols, we did prepare for multiday sweeps, and we brought all our regular operations stuff. After a day or two on operation, I remember one particular night when we had stopped at the top of a hill.

I was again on a late night watch. This time we were on top of a ridge overlooking a beautiful valley. We were somewhere west of the French fort, high in the mountains, looking down a steep drop-off into a rain forest of trees with a river winding around some smaller hills down below. I couldn't see any roads, but I did spot another village at a bend in the river. I could see a few huts, roofs, and a Catholic church spire poking up through the trees. It looked like the opening scene to a Walt Disney movie. There was a full moon to light up the entire area, and that meant there was not a chance in hell that a VC could sneak up this hill because of the expansive grassy area between us and the rain forest below.

I was completely at peace, comfortable, and relaxed. I put the earplugs into my radio and tuned it to Armed Forces Radio. The very first music I heard that night was the theme from The Good, the Bad, and the Ugly. That music seemed to interweave perfectly the unusual combination of sudden scary danger collocated with a beautiful, tranquil Catholic village out in the rain forest. Add to that the ghostly soft whiteness of a full moon hanging over the quiet valley and you had an unreal scenic beauty. Whenever I hear that song, I am transported immediately back to that setting. It may be the most beautiful scene I will ever see, and I will happily keep that memory forever.

It was not always so pleasant, however. On one of those excursions, it rained all day long. Everyone was soaked through to the skin. Everything I owned was soggy, sopping wet. It finally quit raining about sunset, and the skies cleared. It looked to be a nice night, except I was miserably wet. We were all miserably drenched.

We were in the forest, with thick underbrush all around. The word came down that we were stopping and to settle in. As I was heating my beans and franks, I had a great idea. I would empty my pack and spread everything around on the ground so that it could dry out. After that, I had an even better idea. I would strip naked and hang my clothes on the branches all around so that they could drip-dry also. At least they would not be soaking wet in the morning. I'd even wring out my socks and hang them on the branches. Wow, I'd have dry feet.

After eating chow, I unpacked everything and got naked, putting everything on all the branches and bushes in the vicinity. I was lying on my poncho liner looking up at the stars, enjoying my good planning, when I heard, "Saddle up. We're moving out."

Huh?

People were getting up from their spots on the trail and were moving away down the line. I was incredulous. How could this be? We were told that we were stopping and to settle in. Hey, wait for me!

I scrambled to put on as much clothing as I could find and grabbed as much food and belongings as I could in this absolute blackness. I stuffed them into my backpack. The end of the platoon was disappearing down the trail. I picked up my weapon and ran off behind them. As I ran to catch up, I realized that I was Charlie Brown and the USMC was Lucy pulling the football away once again.

I never did find my socks, and I lost half my food. I got food at the next resupply and new socks at another resupply a time or two later. I can tell you that jungle boots do not feel the same without socks.

★★★

In Vietnam, we weren't afraid of dying. We all knew and accepted the possibility that it might happen, of course, but we were not afraid of it because we always saw it as happening to somebody else. We put the possibility of it actually happening to us way down into our subconscious, hidden away in the recesses of our minds. It wouldn't happen to us, and it just wasn't something to dwell on.

And if it did happen, we rationalized that it would happen much, much later—at home in clean white sheets, surrounded by family crying and saying how much we were loved. However, in reality, there was nothing more feared subconsciously than being hit by the ambush or blown up by the mine and dying all alone here in the mud and the slime, covered in blood, or with guts spilling out and never seeing home or loved ones again.

When it did happen, the screams were not because the pain was so unbearable, although it was real and substantial; it was the sudden realization that we had made a *huge* mistake coming to Vietnam.

The man who gets hit like that suddenly realizes that he is actually going to die and it will be here and now, in this rice paddy shit or on this rotting jungle floor, all alone and without family. The terror on his face confirms that he suddenly understands that he will not ever be going home again. He has guessed wrong. He has made a *big* mistake. This was not what he expected. He realizes then that he is going to die … and *soon*. He grasped that he had only a short time left, and his screams were his objections to the unfairness of it.

We did not start out the patrol thinking today was the day that we would be killed. Nevertheless, the threat was always there, lurking in the back of the mind and waiting to come screaming out, unleashing its paralyzing toxins of fear at any unusual sound or sudden movement.

This was just another day out of the old French fort. It may have been a complete company-wide sweep or it may have been only Second and Third Platoons, but this time the Third Platoon had point and Rick Maddy's squad was walking point. We would be up and down in the mountains near the old

French fort. I was in weapons platoon carrying my mortar, and as such, I was fifty or seventy-five yards back of point, closer to Kilo 3 actual and the CP.

It was February 28, 1968, and we were on another normal everyday sweep, nothing any different from any of the others that we had done for months. The events of this day cannot be described any better than by Rick Maddy himself, who wrote this for the website:

> Just another morning in Vietnam. Coming right up was another job for the Corps, the South Vietnamese people, and the beloved people of our country. But something special today. We were going outside the wire in platoon size and spending a few nights out protecting the flank of Highway 1. And we were loaded for bear, as they say in the West.
>
> We walked off our Hai Van Pass hilltop home with a view and onto the paved road leading down the hill and into a fairly tight valley with steep, jagged hills on both sides of the road—possibly the "Bowling Alley." I knew we were east of Hue, toward the South China Sea, but other than that, I knew nothing. A FNG knowing nothing was very common and, I suppose, a good thing.
>
> After walking a bit, a village came into view in front of us. Large artillery shells started to hammer the village, throwing masses of dirt and clods high into the air with the explosions. We took a left off the road and headed toward these wicked-looking hills in front of us. A wild pig darted out across the open rice paddy on my right. We all got a good long look at him. What a magnificent animal, was the thought I had, his white fangs hanging outside the sides of his face, giving their forewarning to anything looking for trouble. His disposition was much like ours: a do not fuck with me—I'm not in the mood—disposition. He was very cool and one of several exotic animals and birds I had seen.
>
> The platoon started the climb up the hill. Several times, I had to put my hand on the ground in front of me or grab a limb of brush for help while we climbed. It was steep and rocky, a real bitch. Finally, after getting through another morning of putting one foot in front of the other, we arrived on top of the ridge sometime around noon. We stopped to eat our portion of C rations. I had been carrying a quart of apple butter someone had stolen from these army guys we had been around a few days before. I had been elected to carry the delicacy. The apple butter was an "accessory" to our food and ammo. A bonus. We ate and prepared to move out along the ridge.
>
> Brisky's fire team, of which I was the newest member, was put on the point. There was lots of brush, almost double canopy. There were tall trees, but you could see the sky and lots of thick, tall brush with some openings. A nice sunny day. Private First Class John Stanford Collier, whom I had never seen before, as far as I could recall, came up to the front and joined the fire team. He was now our point man. Collier was having some difficulty cutting our way through. We were moving very slow, and through the process, we would clusterfuck at times. Second Lieutenant John Ruggles III decided to move forward to help him. The lieutenant and Collier were chopping our way through when we came into this S curve on the trail.

I had no visual contact with the lieutenant or Collier because of the trees and the brush. The first booby trap went off with a ground-moving shock and blur. I immediately hit the deck. Trying to get a better view, I started to crawl forward to look around this tree trunk. I just was getting to the visual when a second booby trap went off. The ground again heaved in a quick blur. This one came with an ear-ringing crack!

I just got a glimpse of Private First Class Robert Aycock as he crumpled off the trail. Private First Class David Brisky was in front of me. We got up at the same time, as did Private First Class Christy "Chief" Goodiron, who was behind me, and Private First Class Sal Negrelli, the lieutenant's radioman behind Chief. I only knew Aycock was hurt and my job was to move forward to help.

Nothing was coming from the lieutenant or Collier. My luck had run out. I took maybe two steps before a third booby trap went off to my left rear. The trap was very close. The device was directly to the front left of Chief. We had been lying on the deck right next to the damn thing and never saw it. I was blown into the air as if doing the standing long jump at a high school track meet. I landed on my feet. On the initial blast, I could see limbs and twigs in front of me snapping off from the shrapnel hitting them. As weird as this may sound, I did not want to fall on my face, so I purposely fell backward.

I felt no pain. I thought I had just taken a hell of a ride through the air from the concussion. I was lying on my pack in what seemed a small open area. My helmet was gone. My rifle was gone. I freaked out. I thought I was going to now be shot to death by gooks involved in this ambush we had just walked into.

I was carrying my usual seven magazines with twenty rounds each for the M16; two or three hand grenades; two bandoliers, with each holding four boxes of twenty round loose M16 ammo; and two belts of M60 machine gun ammo wrapped around me in the Pancho Villa style. Most of the grunts were carrying extra M60 gun ammo for the A-gunner.

There I lay. No weapon. And thankfully no gooks. My ears were ringing so loudly that I couldn't hear anything but Chief screaming. I looked up from my prone position and saw that the top of my right ring finger had been blown off. I caught a glimpse of Brisky thrashing on the ground.

Then there was the crackling of fire. The hot shrapnel had me on fire, and the M60 gun ammo was starting to cook off. I recall at least two or three popping and actually jarring me when they went off. I had to get the pack and ammo off. Panicked, I reached for the pack strap with my right hand, but my arm just flopped along my side with absolutely no control.

I looked down and saw large gaping holes with meat hanging out of my right forearm. No blood. I saw very little blood. Nevertheless, at that moment, I did not realize I had a broken artery in the arm and that I was losing blood quickly. My panic upgraded a bit.

I then tried to use my left arm to get the pack off. I rolled to my right a little. My left forearm swung around, and my hand landed palm down on my face. I could not lift it off my face. I could feel my hand on my face but could not move my hand. Now it went beyond panic. I freaked.

I lifted my head and shook it hard to get the hand off my face. That moment was a creepy feeling, and it still gives me little freak-out thoughts now and then to this day. My hand fell from my face and swung with the arm out to the left. I could see I had dislocated my elbow, or something, by the odd angle of my forearm, and that fucking hand had landed next to me. Now I noticed I was bleeding profusely from my left arm. In reality, the trap had blown my triceps muscle off the back of my left arm and the elbow was completely shattered into small bone fragments.

I was on fire, gun ammo cooking off, bleeding to death, and now came the realization that I was helpless. I needed help. I started screaming for help. I couldn't see anybody. Nobody was around. Words for this moment were difficult to find. Chief, taking the brunt of the trap in the front, had been blown into a tree and had come down in a squatting position, with his back up against the tree's trunk. He was screaming as I have never heard a person scream before. I could see where shrapnel had hit him in the chest and forehead. A small amount of his entrails were hanging out of his right side.

It was sheer horror listening to him. I was yelling and screaming for help, and Chief was just screaming. We were about fifteen feet apart, maybe less. Marines started arriving and swarmed me. Two corpsmen moved forward to help Chief, while the marines started working on Perelli, Brisky, Aycock, and me.

Collier and Second Lieutenant Ruggles were dead.

I was thinking that Chief's screaming was going to give our position away. I yelled at him to shut up. Someone told me to shut up. I have suffered immeasurably my whole life for that moment. I do not know what I was thinking, as if the gooks didn't hear this shit go down miles away or something. I'd made an error in judgment, and I have paid for it. I will forever be sorry that I yelled at him.

I would glance at Chief at times to see how he was doing. He finally settled down and quit yelling and screaming. I heard the air go out of him for the last time, with one long exhale. The time span from first being hit was impossible to tell. I heard the corpsman say he was gone. It was over. The suffering had ended for him. And it had just begun for his family.

I felt someone jerking my left leg around and looked down. Private First Class Daisher was trying to cut my bootstrap off. I told him just to unhook it. He did. I was stripped of my gear and clothing. The marines told me that they needed to sit me up and look at my back. As they sat me up, I was starting to pass out. I had a hole blown in my lower back, just below the beltline, that you could stick the end of a soda can in. They stuffed it and laid me back down. Not one piece of shrapnel had penetrated the flak jacket. I asked for morphine and got it. I told someone to write to my girlfriend and let her know what had happened here if I died.

And now came the wait for the medevac. I knew I was dying. At least it was going to be a painless death. Where was my chopper? I could hear choppers a long ways away on a couple of occasions and asked if that was mine. No. The wounded lay there for over an hour before they brought in a CH-46 to pick us up.

The marines threw me up on the rear ramp while the chopper hovered in the air. No place to land it up there. I will never forget seeing Private First Class Aycock on the chopper shaking his fist at me, glad to see me alive.

The noise was deafening inside the 46. We landed somewhere in Da Nang. They ran me down a long corridor and put me on a cold metal table. There was blood everywhere. Most of it was not mine. A nurse grabbed my head, and we looked at each other upside down. Without words, she turned my head to the side, and I felt the stick of a needle in my neck. Lights out. Now began my "other" tour.

My first two months were in an army hospital's infectious amputee ward in Yokohama, Japan, before being shipped out to the Bremerton Navy Hospital. I would eventually spend a total of almost fourteen months in military hospitals. I had sixteen operations before finally walking out with what was left of me. Both arms had been saved. I was nineteen years old. I was alive.

Private First Class Ronald Christy "Chief" Goodiron: panel 41E, row 066; Private First Class William "Billy" Harris: panel 41E, row 066; Second Lieutenant John Ruggles III: panel 41E, row 072; John Sanforn Collier: panel 41E, row 061

Bastien on a day patrol out of the Old French Fort. The mountains were beautiful. One of these multiday sweeps led us to the ridge overlooking a beautiful Catholic village, where I listened to *The Good, the Bad, and the Ugly* on Armed Forces Radio under a full moon. It was a night I'll never forget.

Lyndon Wilson on a day patrol out of the Old French Fort. The canopy was thick and hid the path. This was full daylight on the trail.

This was an ideal landscape for being ambushed or hitting a booby trap.

ALREADY A LEADER First Lieutenant Fred Smith (second from right), CO of Kilo Company/3rd Battalion/ 5th Marines, gathers with his platoon leaders (left to right) Lieutenants Jack Hewitt, Joe Campbell, and Jack Ruggles, along with Staff Sergeant, later Sergeant Major, Dave Danford (far right) in the Tam Ky area of South Vietnam in the fall of 1967. Lieutenants Campbell and Ruggles were killed in action. Four years later, following a second Vietnam tour, Lieutenant Smith started Federal Express, now FedEx.

Rick Maddy, shortly after graduation from boot camp.

CHAPTER 11

LANG CO

One thing I learned early on about the Marine Corps was that even though tragedy strikes or adversity hinders the task, marines press on through to the objective. When the Marine Corps had an objective, they achieved the objective. The costs were sometimes high. Cost didn't matter. We remained out on operation, sweeping the mountains, clearing the sector, looking for Charlie.

We were now wandering between beaches and highways, from beaches into the mountains and back again. We were now north of Hai Van Pass and south of Troi Bridge, east of Highway 1 and west of the sea. It was cloudy, wet, and cold in the mountains.

The area was still mostly wet jungle rain forest on steep hills, with cliffs and valleys all the way from Highway 1 right down to the beach on the South China Sea. You knew you were getting close to the ocean when the ground leveled off, became white sand, and the trees spread out and became palm and coconut trees. The barrel of your M16 started to rust as you walked.

But in this case, we were up in the hills, where we slept at a forty-five-degree angle on wet weeds with our feet wedged into a tree so we didn't slide downhill during the night. Of course, it rained! It rained all the time now.

March 2 is my birthday. We hadn't seen much action, but then, we hadn't seen much of anything other than the daisy chain booby traps that decimated Maddy's squad and Lieutenant Ruggles. The weather had been really wet. The resupply choppers weren't flying (again), at least not our way.

Rations were low. I was down to a can of jelly, and Jenkins had a pound cake. In honor of it being my birthday, Jenkins offered to share half his pound cake with me for half my jelly. I was getting the better of the deal.

After dark, when we finally stopped, Jenkins and I crawled under our ponchos and prepared for the feast. He opened his can of pound cake, and it did smell good! It was probably WWII pound cake, so how could it still smell good? But it did.

I opened my can of jelly, anticipating the approaching birthday goody. As I peeled the jelly can top back, I couldn't believe what I saw—or, more truthfully, I couldn't believe what I didn't see. *I didn't see any jelly!* What the heck?

There was one little poop of red jelly in that whole can. That was it—only a hint of what should have been in that little can. It looked as if the jelly-canning machine farted its last little squirt of jelly as it ran completely dry at this particular can. Then they closed it up and sent it to me for my birthday!

Jenkins took one look at the empty jelly can and snatched back his pound cake. He gobbled it down fast, right in front of me, before I even had a chance to try to grab it back. When he finished, he smiled his stupid shit-eating grin. It rained on us all that night. I shivered and I was not happy. Moreover, when I woke in the morning, I had slid down the hill about ten or fifteen feet on the wet weeds and was soaking wet.

We continued running operations in the area through February and most of March. Then we were sent down past the old French fort and farther down along Highway 1. We trekked all the way down the mountains from Hai Van Pass to sea level, although the steep mountains were always with us, rising up to those rain forests above. We stopped at a place called Lang Co.

Lang Co was a beautiful little Catholic village located down by the lagoon on one side and next to the ocean on the other. It was nestled among a large grove of tall palm trees, with white sand all around. In those days, it was a small fishing village.

★★★

It was March 31, 1968, in America. In Vietnam, we were waiting for the current occupants of the Lang Co railroad station to vacate so we could move in. Lima Company was taking their sweet time leaving, but that was just fine with me. Because of that, we spent a few days lounging on the white sandy beaches at Lang Co village with nothing to do. Oh, darn the luck.

We pitched our ponchos among the palm trees back from the ocean. During the days, we bartered with kids for Cokes, played cards in the sand, and sat around chatting. It was great—a needed quiet downtime—and if I had been able to take a shower, I would have stayed there forever. But the ocean served well enough for bathing.

At night, I would sit on the beach watching the waves, the stars, and the moon. I would see the waves break and the phosphorescent green created by algae or plankton in the water. It was really quite beautiful, serene, and calming. At night there, it was not too hot and not too cold.

There wasn't a man-made light to be seen. The universe was available for examination, and the Milky Way, with its billions of stars, sat out in front of me over the open ocean. The grandness of the Milky Way hanging so still and clear right out there over the ocean on display hit me like a hammer.

I felt the age of the universe—it had always been and it would always be. It was like looking at infinity. I sensed that it was saying to me that whatever trivial trials and tribulations we humans were creating for ourselves down here, they were nothing to the universe. It seemed to be saying, "You can waste your time fighting all you want, but in the big picture, it won't matter one little bit."

That night, I plugged my earplugs into the radio and tuned to Armed Forces Radio for music. Instead, there was a special news show being broadcasted. I was at the very beginning of it. They were introducing President Lyndon B. Johnson, who was going to make a speech about Vietnam. Hmm, that might be interesting. I wondered what he would say, so I continued to listen, even though it was interrupting my reverie.

I listened to what was a rather boring speech that dragged on and on. I was a twenty-one-year-old kid, not in tune with politics, and I knew only that I would rather be at home in the real world instead of being here in this hot, humid hellhole. He didn't say anything I wanted to hear … until this:

> With America's sons in the fields far away, with America's future under challenge right here at home, with our hopes and the world's hopes for peace in the balance every day, I do not believe that I should devote an hour or a day of my time to any personal partisan causes or to any duties other than the awesome duties of this office—the presidency of your country.
>
> Accordingly, I shall not seek, and I will not accept, the nomination of my party for another term as your president.

But let men everywhere know, however, that a strong, a confident, and a vigilant America stands ready tonight to seek an honorable peace—and stands ready tonight to defend an honored cause—whatever the price, whatever the burden, whatever the sacrifice that duty may require.

Thank you for listening.

Good night, and God bless all of you.

★★★

Huh? What did I just hear? Did that mean the war was over? Were we going home? Was that what he just said? I thought that meant we'd be going home soon. I was excited and hopeful. Could it really be? If he quit, would they bring us home? Well, unfortunately, it turned out that that was *not* what he said and we weren't going home anytime soon. I held on to the hope that we would be going home soon for several days, but it was not to be.

Lima Company did finally leave the Lang Co railway station and turned it over to our responsibility. We packed up from the beach and hiked up to the highway and across to the abandoned railroad station built in a cutout from the cliffs and mountains on the other side of the highway. It was well back from the Catholic ville and beach.

The railway station consisted of three buildings, one of which was the old terminal, completely empty now, lacking any chairs, benches, booths, or ticket counters. It was simply plaster walls and a cement floor. It was long and empty. It became the enlisted quarters. The other two buildings became the command post. I never saw the inside of them.

Therefore, we found ourselves holed up in the Lang Co railway terminal. We made ourselves at home in the terminal and looked around (meaning we dropped the backpacks and weapons). Being in a building was nice for the rain protection, but the floor was uncomfortably hard. I preferred the ground and a poncho.

Outside, there was sheer cliff up the mountain to our backs and a forest of jungle palms and white sand to our fronts, which led to the lagoon and the South China Sea a short distance away.

Marines had been here for some time apparently, although no units remained here for long because it was used as a staging area for more operations and sweeps. But they had made some "improvements" to the area surrounding the three old cement buildings. One of the improvements was an outdoor head for taking your daily dumps. (I have learned since boot camp that *head* in the military means "biffy" for you women and "bathroom" for you other civilians.)

Normally when a grunt needs to take a dump, he simply grabs an E-tool (a small folding shovel strong enough to smash concrete, usually carried on the backpack). He then goes out into the jungle, digs a hole, and squats over it. But that was uncomfortable and messy. It was much better to be able to sit on some type of seat and take a leisurely dump while relaxing, reading a letter from home, or listening to the radio.

Therefore, some ingenious and ambitious second lieutenant (I'm sure) commissioned some grunts to fashion that very thing outside the Lang Co terminal. He had them put together a string of empty fifty-five-gallon drums with the tops removed and then make a supporting bulkhead at each end of the row of empty drums, upon which they put two long steel rails (leftover spare rails for the railroad) that spanned the length of the drums. They now had two supporting rails less than a foot apart, spanning the drums, where somebody could jump onto the rails and sit comfortably, snugly between them, doing their duty and taking a relaxing dump for as long as they felt like it. (A little bit of heaven in South Vietnam.) It supported five or six marines at a time, and the open-air access made it easy to swap out drums as they were filled.

This was my first day here at the station. It came time to do my duty, and that time happened to be about two or three in the afternoon—the hottest time of the day in the sweltering Vietnamese sun. Being more or less used to the high temps, I thought, *Nothing wrong with using the new luxurious head.* It never occurred to me that the metal rails may have absorbed some of the heat of the day. I sauntered out expecting a nice, relaxing dump, contemplating the pretty jungle ahead.

I hadn't been on the steel rails for more than a few seconds before I could hear the sizzling of meat. The smell of burning bacon filled the air. At first, I was a little surprised because I didn't think there was a mess hall here at Lang Co—and, well, there wasn't.

It took just a few more milliseconds for the pain to reach my brain, and I realized it was *me* frying on those rails. I exploded off the rails and landed in the white sand, pants down around my ankles. As I rolled around in agony, I was already wondering if I'd get a Purple Heart for this. A medevac, maybe?

It turned out the Marine Corps did *not* issue Purple Hearts for self-inflicted wounds. And they didn't exactly honor somebody who turned themselves into a human rump roast. So *no*, I did not get a Purple Heart. I did not get medevacked. I did get compliments on my stupidity, though.

We ran daily patrols from the railway station. At night, we swapped off two-hour watches overlooking the station from the cliff behind and above. It was actually nice duty, as we had enough men so that we each only had one watch per night. I don't think that anybody was too worried about a VC attack. The access from above would be very difficult because of the high cliff and steep mountains. Anybody approaching from the road would be highly visible. So only one marine at a time was necessary for watch high above on the cliff.

It came to be my turn. I climbed up the trail, high above the station, and replaced whoever was there on duty. I settled in some tall grass for a two-hour stint and peered out to the South China Sea. In between was that beautiful small village nestled in among tall palm trees, hiding all but the Catholic church spire rising up over them.

I could see past the village that a walking bridge crossed over the lagoon entrance from the ocean to an isthmus on the other side. Over the several nights that I did watch at different times of the night, I noticed the tides coming into the lagoon, raising the water level or leaving the lagoon lowering the water levels. Moreover, I watched the moon over the South China Sea shining down, creating a path of shimmering light on the waves. It was surrealistically beautiful and calming.

I plugged my earphones into the radio. I tuned to Armed Forces Radio. At night, they usually played current music from the States. Sometime during that watch, I'd hear "Love Is Blue," by Paul Mauriat. It fit the scene so perfectly that I will always remember that view, and whenever I hear that song, I will be instantly transported back to Lang Co and that perfect night.

It was not all easy gravy. We still did our patrols. Wilson, Mobeck, Hawthorne, Smitty, and I were told we had the afternoon patrol. We grabbed day-patrol equipment and weapons and started walking up Highway 1 northward toward Phu Bai, leaving the safety of Lang Co behind, not knowing what to expect. We walked a mile or two along the road, facing oncoming traffic. During the day, Highway 1 was packed with buses, trucks, and convoys coming and going in each direction. At night, it was completely empty and desolate.

We came to a nice, easy path from the road up to the top of the cliff that was ten or fifteen feet above us. It was much better to be up there looking down than it was to be down there looking up. We couldn't be surprised from above while we were up on top of the cliff. We continued paralleling the road from above on the cliff for another mile or so, checking the traffic going both ways.

Wilson was leading this motley grimy-looking crew patrolling and guarding Highway 1. It was like an easy stroll in the park. Suddenly, he stopped and said, "Hey, look what I found."

We clustered around to see what he was so excited about. Wilson had found a small mountain spring that had pooled into a small wading pond in the crevice between two bulges of the hill. It was only the size of a bathtub, but it was a pool of clean, cool running water.

Mobeck, ever spontaneous, quickly said, "Let's take a bath."

Now, remember, we had been without showers for weeks. I couldn't remember the last time we had a shower. Before Wilson could say yea or nay to that idea, Smitty and Mobeck were stripped naked. I pulled out my Instamatic camera and snapped a picture of the four of them. Mobeck had brought soap and was already lathered up. He brought soap on a patrol? I never thought to ask him about that later. Smitty was next to lather up. The wading pond was not big enough for more than two at a time. Eventually we all got a turn. To rinse off, somebody pulled a canteen cup out of the canteen holder and opened it up. We filled the cup with cool running water from the stream and drained it over the tops of our heads to get the soap rinsed off. It took a while, but it felt amazing.

It must have been a sight for the buses and trucks passing by, looking up to see naked marines on the cliff top. There was no way they could have seen the stream or wading pond from down there. All they could see were five naked marines pointing and waving at them from the bushes on the cliff. We must have looked like stark raving mad lunatics, which we probably were.

★★★

The days dragged on, one after the other, seemingly always the same day after day. One day, however, we hooked up with Lima Company and went on a large sweep. Suddenly, we had something new and exciting to do. It was something different from the normal grind. We never knew what each new day might bring, sometimes nothing new but sometimes more excitement than we needed. Today however, this was also worrisome because it meant we could very well once again run into unexpected trouble. I'd prefer to leave well enough alone, but that was not the idea with the top brass.

We left at first light and returned late afternoon having seen nobody and experienced no booby traps and no contact. So it was just another day and another job done for the Corps and country. At least we had no casualties. We arrived back at the Lang Co lagoon, which was at low tide now, and afforded us all the opportunity to drop gear, repackage, and regroup it for safekeeping, not locked and loaded anymore.

We were in the process of securing weapons when I heard a loud blast. My head knee-jerked up toward the sound, and down at the other end of the lagoon, I saw a 3.5-inch rocket launcher round going straight up.

What the hell? Somebody fired a 3.5 bazooka round straight up? Why would they do that? And worse, it was gonna come straight down on all these marines. What was going on?

Everybody hit the deck. The round went up and then came down. It smashed into the wet sand but did not explode. It seemed the safety was still attached.

Being in weapons platoon rockets at this particular time in my tour, I also had been carrying a 3.5-inch rocket launcher. I was very curious as to what happened, but from this end of the lagoon, I couldn't see much. There were many people congregating around that marine and the unexploded round.

The 3.5-inch rocket launcher was sometimes called a "super bazooka." It consisted of two tubes, each about two and a half feet long, that were screwed together to make a long hollow tube. It became a big tube about 3.5 inches in diameter. (Duh.)

When you wanted to fire it or if you were on patrol and want to be prepared to fire it, you loaded a rocket round into the back end of the tube. Pulling the trigger sent an electric pulse down to the firing mechanism that fired the rocket. The blast flew out the back end, and the rocket was launched out the front end. Do not be standing behind it.

Doc Sinor was to the scene in a flash. He later told me that a marine had taken the two tubes apart, and the bottom part, with the rocket still in it, was placed on the sand standing straight upward. The marine (for some unknown reason) leaned over it and inadvertently pushed the rocket round down, just a little bit, with his stomach.

That little bit was just enough to create an electrical spark as it moved against the inside of the tube. The rocket ignited and was blasted into the air. This would have been only a stupid fubar and an embarrassment had it not been that the marine was bent over the rocket launcher at the time. The rocket went through the right side of his abdomen. It put a hole in him at least 3.5 inches in diameter.

We sat on the lagoon sand for nearly an hour while they got a chopper to come in for him. The accident put a damper on the otherwise uneventful day. I watched the chopper lift off and head toward Da Nang. We later got word that he didn't make it into Da Nang; he died en route.

I was fortunate to hear from Doc about that accident because I was carrying the exact same weapon. Unpacking after a long, tiring patrol, I realized how very easy it would be to become complacent and make that same fateful mistake. I made a mental note to be extra careful when unpacking the 3.5-inch rocket launcher—complacency kills. Had it not happened to that marine first, it could very well have happened to me. I chalked this up to one of my close calls because I had not thought of this possibility before. I felt saved by that marine's mistake.

★★★

Tet was over but Mini-Tet was being hatched down south of Da Nang in an area known as Dodge City. Dodge City included the vast area south of the 3/5 Battalion area (the home I hadn't seen in months), west to An Hoa, and east to the sea. Farther south of that were mountains. Dodge City, or sometimes referred to as Indian Territory, included a patch of land called Go Noi Island. Although we didn't know it at the time, we were going there, and it would be called Operation Allen Brook. We didn't know it, but 3/27 was getting hammered. We were being called in to help.

Our orders were to stand by the side of Highway 1 until a convoy picked us up for the trip to Hill 55, just south of Da Nang. After a long, uncomfortable, boring day baking in the sun waiting, the trucks finally arrived. We loaded into several "deuce and a half" open-air 6x6 trucks and started on our journey.

I was in the back of one of these trucks, watching the countryside recede into the past. We were leaving behind several more chapters in our adventures there. A blue sky with some puffy white clouds hung over the mountains on the horizon as we barreled down the road. The view I observed brought on a feeling of wanderlust, emptiness, and reflection. Barreling down the road not knowing where I was going pretty much summed up my life to this point.

As the past retreated into memories, the puffy clouds over the mountains beckoned me and seemed to promise opportunity, freedom, and adventure out there on the other side—just beyond and out of reach. I was tied to this truck and the Marine Corps right now, but I sensed that there was opportunity calling that would be available only for a short while longer. It could be missed or lost, just as puffy clouds could become rain clouds or simply dissipate away. My opportunity was still there and still waiting (teasing me, whatever it was), but I had to go get it. It would not wait forever, and it would not come to me.

This was my first serious yearning to get back home and to become engaged in something of value, something worthwhile. I realized that time was wasting and opportunity was moving past at an alarming rate, much as the countryside was flashing past us in this truck. I was still only half stepping through life. I needed to determine some future directions and goals.

I stared at the openness down the road and wondered where it would eventually lead me and what I would do when I got there. I could tell that there was something out there, pending and waiting. I knew that there was still more to do in this life—something more to accomplish and more to see. I just didn't have a clue what it was. I'd leave that to happenstance.

Lyndon Wilson, Don Mobeck, and Anthony Weiber, all from weapons platoon, on a day operation out of Lang Co. It was always hot and humid.

Vincent on a day patrol up and behind Lang Co. It was beautiful country there, and you could see the Lang Co lagoon in the distance.

Smitty starting to lather up, Hawthorne and Wilson waiting their turn, and Mobeck already fully lathered in our mountain stream bath

This was the first "bath," or "shower," we had had for weeks.

Barreling down the road not knowing where I was going pretty well sums up my life to this point.

The clouds on the horizon and the big open spaces there and beyond beckoned with a promise of opportunity and adventure. I just had to go grab it.

CHAPTER 12

PHU BAI

We departed Lang Co for Go Noi Island and Operation Allen Brook. There we burned through the end of May, June, and part of July clearing the enemy from land that had been cleared before and would need to be cleared again by future marines. It seemed to me that we weren't serious about keeping territory won with the blood of my friends. Nobody had explained any goals or objectives to me, and as far as I could tell, not to any of my buddies either. I didn't see any plans or any objectives. I was not privy to the information of the planners and shakers, but I saw nothing of value happening and nothing worth losing lives over. I certainly didn't know what we were doing or why. We just did and died.

Sometime in July, we abandoned Go Noi Island. The unit had survived Operation Allen Brook, although not all of us had survived it and not all of us were uninjured. Some had been shipped home in bags. Some had been medevacked home on hospital ships or airplanes. But that time and that operation were now over, in the past. The rest of us remained. It was now into July 1968, and we moved north again, this time all the way to Phu Bai. This was the new battalion home.

Phu Bai was a city just north of the very end of the Bowling Alley. It was located just a few miles southeast of Hue City, which became famous during the Tet Offensive. The Battalion area included an air base.

Looking to the southeast, there was a long valley that somewhat had the appearance of a bowling alley. From Phu Bai, Highway 1 runs generally southeast back to the mountains that make up the bowling pins. Facing southeast, the South China Sea was on our left (east side), and the range of inland mountains that rose into that beautiful rainforest was on our right.

Way down the line, Lang Co was the last village before starting up the climb past the old French fort to Hai Van Pass. Kilo Company was spread out throughout this valley, assigned to protect the many bridges that crossed the rivers flowing down from the mountains.

Third platoon was being sent to Claymore Pass, a hill about half way to Lang Co, where we would stage patrols. The hill sat high above the highway and had a good view of the coastal valley all the way to the mountains at the end. It was situated such that the big lagoon that reached Lang Co was directly in front when facing northeast to southeast, and the mountains were to the south and southwest on our right. The other platoons of Kilo Company were spread out and stationed at individual bridges along the way or they remained in Phu Bai.

Our platoon traveled in 6x6s to our hill. We found the trail, and up we went. The jungle there was dense, with tangled vegetation all around and down here at sea level; the forest was thick with vines. It would be very difficult to climb this hill were it not for the trail. The trail was winding, narrow, and steep. It eventually brought us to the top and then continued around the hill.

Mobeck, Hawthorne, Wilson, Jenkins, Baltes, and I were at the tail end of this party. When we finally broke through the forest and climbed out into the sunshine, the entire parade stopped. The point had reached the end of the trail. We had almost completely circled the top. The trail was filled up with a few marines spread out at about twenty-five-yard intervals. Word was passed down that where you were was where you stayed. Dig in. We happened to be located at the only entrance to our hilltop abode. The entire hill below us was surrounded by a wall of very dense forest and scrub brush.

Wilson, Mobeck, Jenkins, and I decided to combine ponchos and make a four-man hooch. Baltes and Hawthorne moved up the line to make their own accommodations farther from our hilltop entrance. We created a nice fighting and listening hole right in front of our four-man hooch. We filled the hooch with dry straw-like weeds from the hill. Adding little ditches along the sides to keep the rain from rolling through made our new home the best possible, given our conditions. It was about as comfortable and as accommodating as I have seen made out of ponchos and sticks.

I took a group picture of us. We were a motley crew of misfits, certainly not the dress blue marines back on embassy duty in the capital. We were the Third Platoon "Rough Riders."

After settling in, one of the first directives issued was by some dipstick officer in the rear who decided it would enhance his résumé if he could show that we commanded the area at night. To secure that image, we would patrol Highway 1 via jeep with four infantrymen and a machine gun. They would drive up to the Bowling Alley—past all the villages, bridges, and rivers—and then return to Phu Bai each night.

From my perch overlooking the valley, I could see the taillights almost all the way to Lang Co and the headlights almost all the way back. I didn't think that this plan was a good idea, and I knew that I surely did not want to be in that jeep. You could see and hear the jeep for miles. Everyone knew where it was all along the entire trip.

The foolish operation continued for three or four nights, and then they were ambushed, just as we all expected. I don't remember the outcome of the jeep drive-by ambushing, but the night operation was discontinued and never reinitiated.

We ran several patrols and ambushes nightly from our hilltop station. Those of the Rough Riders not out on patrol or ambush formed the defense against any intrusion from below coming up the hill.

Jenkins and I got the watch that night because Wilson and Mobeck were out on night patrol or at another hole around the perimeter. We guarded the only entry point between the path up the hill, and the remainder of the unit scattered around the top.

This was a scary place to be. There had been a considerable number of firefights in the area. The monkeys hated us (for some unknown reason), and they liked to sneak up at night and throw rocks at us. Of course, the incoming thud made by a rock hitting the ground sounded exactly like an incoming grenade ready to explode. We had to hit the deck every time, and I could just imagine those monkeys laughing their asses off at us. There was also a report in the *Stars and Stripes* newspaper about a marine who had been dragged off his hillside hole one night by a tiger, not too far from where we were and not too long ago.

Another fun fact of this place was that the longer that we stayed on this hill, the farther down the hill marines had to travel to do their duty. They traveled with E-tool in hand to dig their poop hole and squat over it. We had to go deeper into the forest each night to do our duty. One night a marine went down into the trees and squatted over his hole with pants down around the ankles. Just then he saw a bear! For real.

He came scrambling back up the hill with pants still down around the ankles, yelling, "Don't shoot. Marine here!" He had literally had the shit scared out of him. Unfortunately, the dumb bear later came up the hill right into our lines and was killed.

Tonight Jenkins and I were the sentries at the only entry point where the only path up the hill met our path around the hilltop. To get to the rest of the platoon from down below, you had to go through us.

The path in front of us was completely black. You couldn't see a thing, even though it was only feet away. The terror of not being able to see anything, being reliant on hearing only, and knowing the bad guys were out there trying to get to you was beyond description. The fear was insidious. It grew as time passed. It built up. It got to the point where sometimes something would have to *pop*.

That's the reason so many vets say, "You had to be there" (to know what it was like), and they got so frustrated when trying to explain. Conveying the complete context is usually impossible.

Jenkins got first watch. I crawled into the poncho tent and tried to fall asleep on our nice straw floor. Jenkins stared into the abyss of blackness, listening. It was completely still and quiet except for an occasional burst of gunfire far off across the valley. The occasional burst of gunfire far away was reminiscent of the lonely dog at night, back home, barking across the field or several blocks away in the quiet darkness, looking for company, or more likely, frightened at something moving in the shadows.

Jenkins was a skinny black kid from Louisiana. Although he was a bit high strung and a nervous type, when he was relaxed he loved to use words to paint verbal pictures of things like a cool, moist can of ice-cold beer or his favorite parts of the female human body. He was a real team player and would stand by anyone in trouble at any time. He was a good friend to have (even though he didn't share his pound cake with me on my birthday). Jenkins was a guy to like because he tried to be a friend and wanted to be a friend. He would stand with you, but he really did not want to be here. He was always a bit nervous and jumpy.

I was trying to convince my body to sleep when I heard Jenkins say in a shaky trembling voice, "Basteeeen? Come out here!"

He sounded scared, and I thought, *That doesn't sound good.*

I rousted myself up and crawled to the front of the poncho tent. I stuck my head out to see what was going on, and I saw Jenkins, with a shaky finger, pointing at a large glowing orange parachute jumping around in the night sky just out in front of us. "What the hell is that?" he asked in a high, tight, squeaky voice.

I had never seen anything like it. I was wondering what the heck that could be. Without waiting for me to reply, he said, "I'm gonna shoot that motherfucker," and he fired off a burst of rounds.

I saw the tracers disappear into the glowing orange parachute and said, "You got it!"

But nothing happened. It just sat there floating in front of us, bouncing around.

The sound of shots fired disturbed those on the other side of the hill, and we could hear them stirring, probably coming to investigate. We sat there wondering what this thing was. I was also wondering what we would say about this unauthorized giving away of our position when Jenkins and I both noticed something very interesting, very disturbing, and something calming at the same time.

The clouds above us and in front of us were beginning to break apart now and showing much more open night sky than before. We noticed that the wind was blowing the clouds past us quickly. And we noticed through one of the new large clear patches of night sky that a full moon was just now rising over the tops of the mountains to our southeast.

Our large glowing orange parachute was actually a full moon just halfway risen over the mountains out in front of us! It had seemed to be jumping about because of the fast-moving clouds racing by. Jenkins had shot at the moon, and I had thought that he had hit it!

When the others arrived from around the other side of the hill, I didn't want to admit that Jenkins was shooting at the moon, so when they asked, I said, "Jenkins thought he heard something."

The lieutenant was livid and responded, "Damn it. When you hear something, throw a grenade at it or they'll know where you're at!"

Jenkins was now so relieved at determining what his dangerous foe was that he had no inhibitions about blurting out, "Yup, now the moon know where I at."

Everyone dispersed back to their hooches and holes on the trail, and things settled down. But Jenkins was still shaking. He was quite rattled. Actually, he was a mess. He said, "I need a drink."

He crawled into the hooch and found his nice big bottle of whiskey that he'd just brought back from R & R. He had just gotten been back a few days ago. He gulped down a bunch of it in just a few minutes. He soon became completely wasted and useless. Although I spent the rest of the night on watch myself, I felt somewhat sorry for him. He had just come back after being gone for a week and getting his mind back to "normal." And here he was once again, traumatized right from the get-go. Welcome back to the Nam!

It was later in the month, I think. We had relocated off our hilltop home and had gone on bridge watch. Our bridge was somewhere between Lang Co and Phu Bai and close by our recent hilltop home on Claymore Pass. It was between one bridge farther up toward Phu Bai and another bridge farther down toward Lang Co.

The bridge we were "saving" crossed a good-sized river running down from the mountains to our west and flowed to the ocean a mile to the east. Our purpose was to keep the bridge intact, not allowing it to be destroyed which stopped traffic and commerce. Cronen's squad had the northeast quadrant, with Highway 1 on our left and the river on our right. I was assigned to this squad.

The center of our camp was at the intersection of the bridge and the river. We had a lookout bunker twenty-five yards up the road and twenty-five yards down the river, toward the ocean. There was a sandbag "wall" that stood about four feet high and was curved from one bunker to the next in a ninety-degree arch. In our perimeter, there were three or four sandbag hooches. Down by the river was one nice big tent that housed army engineers. I had no idea what they were doing there.

Two nights ago was a nice night, and during that clear night, we watched and listened as the bridge to the south of us had a nasty firefight that lasted a good long while.

Last night was a cloudy and somewhat rainy, windy night, and we watched and listened as the bridge to the north of us had a nasty firefight that lasted a good long while.

Today was a nasty, rainy, and windy day. We had been warned that a typhoon was inbound. The weather would get bad. I figured, *Great—all the better for the bad guys to sneak over our wall and attack.* Rumors and theories ran rampant with everybody speculating that we'd be hit tonight. It was our turn, and the weather would be perfect for a sneak attack. We were ramped up on adrenaline and dread.

As the day passed, it got dark and the weather became horrendous. We were all nervous. The wind howled. The rain pelted our sandbag hooches. The river rose and got big, fast, and violent. During the night, it eventually washed away the overlaps that connected the bridge to the road, making the bridge unusable, but the bridge remained intact. The rising river swallowed the army tent, and it came down. We lost radio communications with all the other quadrants. We were on our own.

We huddled in our little sandbag houses, expecting an attack. We were locked and loaded, ready for anything. We sat waiting on cots and ammo boxes. Waiting is the hardest on the nerves. The mind wanders, anticipating the worst. Any sudden noise or movement is the thing that can trigger you to reflexively spring into action—warranted or not, wise or not. Waiting builds anticipation, which causes dread, which can cause a knee-jerk reaction. Only action relieves tension.

I thought I'd better make the rounds of our two lookout bunkers. I needed something to do to release the tension. I headed out into the raging storm and approached the bunker by the road. Steve Cronen was on watch in it. He was apparently a "little" nervous also because as I approached from his rear, he heard me and swung around with his M16 pointed directly at me, eyes as round as silver dollars. He came within a millisecond of pulling the trigger.

We exchanged pleasantries (profanities, actually), and I proceeded down to the other lookout, which was nearly swamped by the rising river. This time I announced well in advance that I was inbound to check on things. I returned to my hooch soaked to the skin. This time I shivered from cold and nervous tension.

Then it happened!

I just got in the hooch and sat down on an ammo box, and we heard a muffled *bang* from what sounded exactly like a hand grenade going off in the hooch next to us. Then there was a muffled scream from a marine in that hooch. We all looked at each other like "Here we go. This is it. This is the Alamo."

I was closest to the door, so out I went, fully loaded, ready to meet my maker. I felt as if I was Davy Crockett at the Alamo, and I was not going down without a fight. I hit the storm full on, wind at hurricane strength, rain going sideways, the river almost up to our area. The bridge had already been rendered unusable, and the engineer tent was flat on the ground.

The first thing I saw was a newspaper blowing in the wind, coming straight at me quickly. It was almost upon me. I was confused. Who was reading a newspaper out here in the storm at this time of night? I reflexively shot the shit out of it with my M16, and a thousand little pieces of paper flew right by me.

Now everybody was sure that there were gooks over the wall and they had infiltrated our little corner. They didn't know if that was incoming or outgoing fire, but it must be bad news either way. There was no time to dwell on why a newspaper was attacking me. Where were the bad guys? We were all walking around looking. I was screaming, "Don't shoot! Marine here!"

We couldn't find any bad guys, but the marine was still screaming in a muffled voice. That's when we realized that the hooch next door wasn't there anymore. The hooch next door had collapsed. It was made of plastic sandbags that became slippery when wet, not the nice canvas sandbags that never moved once they were set in place. The screaming marine was under hundreds of sandbags in what was once his hooch, and we were walking all over him trying to find him.

We finally found him and got him into one of the remaining hooches. He had to wait a day until the weather cleared enough for the medivac helicopter to come pick him up. There was not much that could be done for his broken leg. Doc gave him some Darvon or maybe something even a little stronger.

After that incident, we begin to relax a little. We really didn't need to fear an attack; the NVA wouldn't be out in this storm either!

★★★

Steve Cronen had been my friend since the first day I got in the country. He greeted me at the 3/5 Battalion area and showed me the ropes. We were at CAP III together and did patrols together. I was with him the night we walked through the gook ambush at the beginning of Tet at Anderson Bridge. We'd just gone through a typhoon together. It seemed as if he couldn't get rid of me, and vice versa.

All this time, I had been in "rockets." That means I was a regular grunt usually, except that I was part of weapons platoon and was assigned out to different platoons, depending on their needs. As a rockets guy, I carried and fired the 3.5-inch rocket launcher or a LAAW. The LAAW is pretty cool and a lot easier to carry than the super bazooka—nearly the same power but much lighter. I could carry three of them myself.

This morning I was scheduled to go out on patrol with Cronen and his squad. We'd leave the bridge and cross over Highway 1, out past the lagoon. We'd find the old railroad tracks out close to the ocean. Then we'd follow that for a while and make sure there were no bad guys planning anything nasty. Then we'd come home to a delicious (ha!) dinner of C rations ham and lima beans.

I was getting saddled up, ready to go. Sergeant Brown came over to me and said, "Basteen, you're staying here today. You're gonna learn mortars."

I said, "Okay," not unhappy about missing a patrol.

Cronen and his squad departed, and I went over to an open area with the sergeant and met Hawthorne, who was also going to learn mortars. We spent most of the day learning to tear down the mortar (not much to it), clean it, reassemble it, and how to set it up. Then we learned about aiming it, determining how to decide the elevation of the tube and how many increments to use on the rounds, depending on range desired. We learned about the range card.

Overall, it was an interesting day. The lessons took up most of it. I was pleased to be getting away from rockets and into something new and more interesting. I didn't realize this would mean carrying heavier equipment, but I was content for now.

Word arrived that Cronen's team had stepped on a mine or some other booby trap. They were walking in a train tunnel, and somebody tripped it. One was dead, one was alive but had lost his legs, and others were injured. They were all medevacked out by helicopter, but nobody at the CP knew who was dead, who lost their legs, or what the other injuries were to the others. We'd have to wait to find that out. This was one of the few times that I became really upset. Usually cool, I lost it.

I wasn't with them. I was aghast, frightened, and terribly distraught. I was supposed to be on that patrol. Maybe I could have helped. Maybe I could have seen the trap. I felt as if I had deserted them. I should have been there. Now what? What happened to Steve? It was a personal hell to sit and wait, unable to help, unable to do anything, and not knowing their status.

It was happenstance that I was picked to learn mortars that day. I didn't choose it. It just happened. I guess I was glad that I was chosen, but I had survivor's guilt. I should have been there.

Wilson, Baltes, Mobeck, Jenkins, and Hawthorne at our hooch on Claymore Pass. The four-man luxury poncho tent was populated by Wilson, Mobeck, Jenkins, and me.

Jenkins, with his R & R whiskey, was sitting exactly where he was when he tried to shoot the moon. I was sticking my head out of the poncho tent, advising him that he hit it.

Wilson, Mobeck, and Bastien at the only entrance from the trail through the vegetation up to the marines at the top of Claymore Pass.

This was the view from our hooch and was the view Jenkins and I had when we were terrified by that glowing orange parachute that turned out to be the moon rising over the mountains in the far distance, just over where the helicopter was.

That helicopter and landing pad was actually a long way away and quite far down the hill. The vegetation in the foreground was actually tops of forest trees and our trail winds down through it.

This may be Troy Bridge or Bridge 13. Bridge duty was nice, as we could go swimming and there was a village where we could get a beer during the day. This was *not* the bridge where we were when the typhoon hit.

When we left this area, we walked alongside this river, upstream toward the mountains. About a mile upstream, I glanced down to the river and saw an alligator swimming in it, looking for dinner.

Here in Phu Bai, we could wash clothes and quickly dry them on those metal roofs. Phu Bai had showers, a mess hall, and an enlisted men's club. It was good duty there. Unfortunately, it was short but sweet. Tom Alexander is sitting—Don Mobeck, Lyndon Wilson, and Anthony Weiber standing.

Larry Jones, a friend from San Diego MCRD boot camp who happened to be passing through Phu Bai with Lima at the same time that Kilo was there. We had met up once or twice previously on Operation Allen Brook.

CHAPTER 13

OPERATION MAMELUKE THRUST

There was not much happening up here on Highway 1 anymore. We had secured the route from Hai Van Pass to Phu Bai. Patrols were not finding much resistance. The bridges were rebuilt after the typhoon. We encountered only booby traps and snipers but no large engagements with Charlie. He was overwhelmed by sheer brute force and had decided not to battle overwhelming odds.

Down south near An Hoa, however, more operations were brewing. The brass was looking for fresh meat to insert into Operation Mameluke Thrust. They needed more people. Therefore, we were moved up to the Phu Bai Combat Base for air transport to An Hoa, where our new operations would begin. They must have wanted us there yesterday, because we were flying instead of walking. We loaded into the belly of a C-130. The C-130 was a four-engine turboprop multipurpose aircraft currently configured empty for the purpose of carrying cargo, namely us.

Walking up the rear ramp, we entered a cavernous empty bay. There were no seats, no seatbelts, and no flight attendants. There was a lone crew chief standing between us and the hatch into the pilot's compartment, probably to keep us from hijacking the plane to Cuba, I guess. There were no windows, or if there were, I couldn't see them. So we sat with all our combat gear, squashed together like kindergarten children playing Duck, Duck, Gray Duck.

The four engines started and screamed so loudly that I was afraid I'd lose my hearing. I noticed that the crew chief was wearing a headset. The back ramp closed, and now it was dark. There may have been a few yellow lights scattered around along the walls. This increased my dread and apprehension. I normally might be scared, but now I was simply insanely angry at the loud engine noise. I couldn't even talk to the guy sitting squashed right next to me, and the screaming engines were damaging my ears.

We turned and rumble bumped down a taxiway, turned onto a temporary runway, and accelerated for takeoff. The entire runway was made of steel plates buckled or zipped together like the zipper on Wrangler jeans. The takeoff roll down the steel plates was rough and bouncy. It felt as if the wheels would be torn off.

These temporary runways were actually called Marston Mats, more properly called pierced (or perforated) steel planking (PSP), and were standardized perforated steel matting material developed by the United States shortly before World War II. An airport could be made quickly with these.

Takeoffs and landings in Vietnam were all steep and short, using the short-field technique. You needed to get away from the ground as fast as possible, and you needed to get down onto the ground as quickly as possible. It was not a comfortable or reassuring ride. It was probably better that I couldn't see outside.

Only fifteen or twenty minutes later, we arrived in An Hoa. We landed at the air base after steep turns and a descent that reminded me of the E rides at Disneyland. My hearing recovered, and my stomach rejoined my body. I was still mad about the noise. We got resupplied and refurbished. We'd be leaving tomorrow in the morning. We would sweep and search once again as we pressed on through our area.

Intelligence said that there was a division of NVA staging in these forests. This was the best distance for rocket attacks on Da Nang. It was called the rocket belt. There had already been fighting, and we'd join it.

After being deployed and early on in our operation, word came down that we were changing our mode of operation. We would now move at night with the intent of catching them by surprise. At about sunset, we stopped as per usual and had our C rations dinner. But we did not set up the poncho tents. We remained packed and ready to move out.

A little later, it started to rain. Just after that, word was passed that we were moving out. The dark cloudy, rainy night hid everything. It started to pour. It rained and rained. It rained hard. I didn't know how point could stay on the rice paddy dike in the darkness, let alone know where he was going. The rice paddies filled with water, and the ground and dikes became soft and squishy. Clothes were soaked through and through. Cold water was running down my back. My vision was blurry because of the rain streaming down across my glasses. It was like looking through the glass block wall that sometimes surrounds a bathroom shower at home for that decorative look.

It was late. I was tired, but we continued slogging through the mud. I was soaking wet and cold. I couldn't see anything past the guy in front of me. My fingers were white, wrinkled, and useless. They were wrapped around the barrel of my mortar tube, which was slung over my left shoulder along with the attached baseplate. We humped like this through the pouring rain for what seemed like hours, single file and closer together than normal simply to keep from becoming separated.

Then, just as we always anticipated, we received incoming small arms fire from the tree line on our left. I saw the flashes and heard the cracks from the weapons being fired at us. Fortunately for me, it appeared to be quite a bit farther forward. I really didn't want to get down into this muddy rice paddy shit, and the firefight seemed way up ahead, so I just stood there waiting for it to be done. Firefights were generally over in less than a minute.

Those with M16s up ahead got down and returned fire. I had a 60 mm mortar and a .45-caliber handgun; not much I could do unless this got serious. So I just stood and waited until it was over and figured we'd press on later.

As I thought, the firefight was over as soon as we returned fire. There was no more gunfire from the tree line. They were gone. It was simply a hit-and-run attack, probably by a few of the local VC from one of the many villages in this area. I heard a marine from about two guys forward of me yell, "Corpsman, up!"

Huh? I moved forward to see what he was yelling about. I saw a marine down in the mud. He was only two guys ahead of me. The firefight that had seemed so far ahead was only two men forward of me. A corpsman arrived, and they started working on him, surrounding him and holding a poncho over him so the corpsman could work on him. This reminded me of Tim McGuire back during Allen Brook.

The rest of us were told to spread out and form a perimeter. While I was on the perimeter, it stopped raining but it was still very dark and cloudy. We all remained wet and cold. When the medevac chopper arrived, they popped some flares to mark the landing area and he was loaded onto his lifeboat out of there. For the remainder of that night, the rain was on and off and never seemed to end. I don't remember the sunlight coming out after that.

After that night, our new nighttime adventures were discontinued. I guess it didn't work out so well and the surprise was on us rather than on them. Of course, most of us weren't surprised at all.

I don't know if this counted as a narrow escape because although it was close (to me), if I had gotten hit, it would have been because of my own stupidity for not getting down. I decided to consider it a half close call and half stupidity. It didn't matter anymore, though, because I had lost count of the close calls and it was too late to start counting stupidity, as I had already made a large number of them.

★★★

Ron Heath was given the nickname "Pack Rat" because he was a collector and wanted to bring a museum full of NVA items back home with him. Therefore, at every opportunity, he picked up and carried anything NVA that he could find. The number of items just kept getting bigger and bigger.

He had an AK-47 rifle, an NVA flag, a bunch of NVA maps, the cover (hat) of an NVA officer, one or more NVA canteens, and probably a lot of other stuff I can't even remember. He carried it along with all the Marine Corps stuff he was supposed to have, as well as the extra C rations that he had stolen from unwary grunts. His pack was huge. Standing up with the pack on his back, he looked as wide as he was tall.

He was built fairly stout, kind of like a bulldog, and had somewhat broad shoulders with stronger-than-average arms, so he was built for carrying a lot of stuff. He usually wore a fun-looking smiling round face and a balding head (already bald in those days at that young age was weird, not like today). To look at him made you smile (or even laugh), and you couldn't help but like him.

Ron Heath was the butt of a lot of jokes and ribbing, but he was one of the smartest men in our unit. He had been sent to language school at one time and was good at interviewing Vietnamese villagers or POWs. He came to us from another unit as a weapons platoon squad leader. After his stint in the marines, he would become a respiratory technician and live in Alaska for many years before moving to Southern California to finish his career and then retire. Heath was smart, had a great memory (or imagination), and was very friendly … I'd call him "a good guy."

One time we stole some of his C rations chow simply because he was hoarding it and we had run out. This was one of the few times he ever got angry. We never admitted to him who did it, and for forty years he blamed me, until a few years ago, when Steve Cronen finally fessed up. Of course, it was really no big deal because he simply went and stole somebody else's.

One day we were out on operation and walking through some open rice paddy areas. Usually there was only one dike (a little dividing wall between the paddies), and we used to walk on those, single file and spread out about every ten to fifteen yards or so. This day, however, there happened to be two dikes running parallel, separating the rice paddies. The dikes were about a foot and a half apart, and that made a nice trough, probably for diverting or directing water, and if it had been wet, there would have been water in there. But today it was bone dry.

Both dikes were being used by our marines. Suddenly, I heard a yell for help from behind me a little way back. I turned to look, and there in the trough between the dikes was Pack Rat Heath on his back and wedged into the trough. He looked like a turtle that somebody had flipped on its back, legs and arms flailing wildly.

Wilson, Cronen, and I all went back to see what had happened. Pack Rat said, "I slipped off the dike and fell into this ditch … I can't get up." He had one of those huge backpacks (for carrying 3.5-inch rocket rounds) that was completely filled and attached to everything he owned.

"Well, if you didn't have such a big pack, you might be able to sit yourself up."

We all laughed and pointed as other marines just continued walking past. We said, "Have a nice day." We walked away.

Later, when we had stopped and taken a break, he caught up with us. We never found out if another marine helped him up or if he wiggled out of that pack and got himself up. We never talked about it again until a few years ago at one of the reunions. The following is an account by Heath of that day, plus or minus some of the details.

> The Marine Corps was not in the business of dealing in off-the-rack clothing. I became painfully aware of this in 1968. Jungle utilities, because of their light weight, were always tearing or getting just plain worn out in a hurry. It was just part of the territory. Jungles were forests of thorns and snagging branches that would stress even the toughest Levi's.
>
> Whenever we were resupplied, we would receive a few sets of new jungle utilities. These were usually given out to the men most in need of clothing (read that as dressed in ragged utilities). After one particularly nasty patrol, I fell into that category. The supply chopper had come and gone, and we went to see what the people in the rear had sent us for clothing. There were the usual large/long trousers (thirty-eight-inch waist and thirty-six-inch inseam) and a few medium/regulars (thirty-four-inch waist and thirty-four inch inseam).
>
> At that time (I wish it were so today), I was what was referred to as a short/small (twenty-nine-inch waist and twenty-eight-inch inseam). There were none of these to be had in the current resupply, so I had to make do with medium/regular.
>
> Thank God for the Marine Corps brass buckle and web belt. I had my belt pulled as tight as I could get it to keep my trousers up. Having the crotch of your trousers showing is fashionable today, but in those days it was an irritation.
>
> Word was passed to saddle up for patrol, so I put on my cartridge belt and bandoleer. I just couldn't seem to keep my trousers up high enough to get a good walking stride. This I could live with. However, when the time came to jump a ditch between one rice paddy dike and another, that was all she wrote. No sooner had I made my leap than I heard the ominous ripping sound. There was a large tear along the seam at the crotch.
>
> Well, it's not as if I was in civilization, where people would stare or anything, so I just hitched 'em up and kept moving. After a short while, word was passed back to get off the trail and take a break. It was early morning, the sun had only been up a couple of hours, and the heat of the day hadn't started yet. I looked around for a comfortable place to sit and saw a small mound next to the trail and sat down. I relaxed and began brushing the rust specks off my rifle with my toothbrush.
>
> Then it started, slowly at first. It was just an itching and tickling sensation. Then they attacked. They had crawled into the hole in the crotch of my trousers and were biting my balls. They were everywhere, and they were the tiniest ants I had ever seen. It had been my misfortune to choose their nest as my seat during the rest break.

I was a lot wiser in selecting my seat after that. I also began keeping a spare pair of short/small trousers in my pack.

★★★

I have only had three fights in my life. These fights were not about life or death; they were about ego, self-image, and status among peers.

My first fight was in the second grade, with the neighbor kid from across the street, who was a whole year older than I was. We got into a tussle. I don't remember why. We met in the middle of the street, threw a few punches, and then he landed one right on my nose. I had a bloody nose, so I went home ("loss").

Then, in the eleventh grade, I was walking home one winter day from high school with a buddy in my class, along with his older brother, both behind me. We were cutting across a field single file in the snow in mid-January, walking on the narrow path through the snow. *Whap!* A snowball hit me in the head. I turned around and they were laughing. I couldn't have that, so I told them to stop it … or else.

We took a few more steps and *whap!* Another snowball in the back of the head. I turned around to face Bob Bursch. We threw a few punches. However, our parkas were so big and heavy that neither one of us could land anything that hurt the other. Soon we were huffing and puffing. I said, "I'll quit if you do."

He did ("tie").

In Vietnam, Hawthorne and I had been thrown into the same 60 mm mortar squad. Ideally, there were four people in a squad: the squad leader, the gunner, the ammo humper, and the second ammo humper. I worked my way up the chain of command simply by surviving long enough. I was currently gunner and carried the .45 caliber and the mortar. Hawthorne was a few days later getting in country than I was, so I had seniority and he was ammo humper.

Our squad leader, who I think was Wilson at the time, was able to return home or was reassigned elsewhere. I didn't know, but I was suddenly the new squad leader. That meant I would now carry no tube or baseplate. Good news! The gunner would normally haul the .45 pistol and the mortar.

I should not be carrying that heavy gun anymore, and Hawthorne, who had suddenly been promoted out of ammo humper, would no longer be carrying heavy mortar rounds and a cumbersome M16. There was a new guy who became the new ammo humper. We had long ago lost the second ammo humper, and he was never replaced. I don't know if I ever knew the name of this new guy, but if so, I have long since forgotten it.

So we were rich with the power of a better position and less weight to carry (at least I was). We were down to three, but it was still a promotion!

Then, the next day, our new guy was shot and medevacked out of there. That left only Hawthorne and me. As mentioned before, Hawthorne was of Mexican descent from San Antonio, Texas. He was a good guy, with a very distinctive Hispanic and fun accent. For example, his word for *jeep* was *jip*. He was usually fun to be around. Hawthorne had a habit of smoking a lot of weed, and he did not have a fondness for "the Man," but he got along great with us "blue-collar" workers.

It was morning and the company was moving out, back into sweep mode. I told Hawthorne to "saddle up, pick up the ammo, let's go."

He said, "I'm gunner. I'm not humping that ammo."

I reminded him, "It's just you and me now. I'm squad leader *and* gunner. You are the ammo humper *and* the second ammo humper. Pick up the ammo. Let's go."

Suddenly, in his eyes, I was "the Man," and there was opposition. He said, "No, you hump it. I'm not gonna do it."

Now *this* was decision time. I would never have any credibility or respect if I let this mutiny stand. I must stop this now. I started toward him. He jumped up on an ammo box and leaped on me. We were both fully loaded with canteens, backpacks, helmets, weapons, and so on. We were ready to leave *except* that one of us would carry the gun and one of us would carry the ammo.

We were rolling around in the dirt of our makeshift mortar pit, and the rest of the company was passing us by, smiling and laughing at the two stupid grunts wrestling in the dirt. The captain walked by and said, "Basteen, is there a problem here?"

Amazingly, we both stopped wrestling for a moment while I replied, "No, sir. Private Hawthorne and I are having a discussion about load sharing."

He said, "Carry on," and continued walking.

We resumed wrestling. I could feel that I had the advantage now because I had wrestled in high school; Hawthorne obviously had not. I had Hawthorne on his stomach and his right arm in a "chicken wing," bent around behind his back. And that hurts. I was pushing him around the mortar pit on his face, and he was getting a bunch of scratches and eating a lot of dirt. He looked like a snowplow in a Minnesota blizzard.

Finally, he yelled out, "Okay, okay, I'll carry the ammo."

Victory at last ... a *win* for the good guy!

I jumped up off him, picked up the mortar and baseplate, and joined the rest of the company before he had any chance to change his mind. Hawthorne picked up the ammo and rejoined the company. We never said another word about it. I have now retired from fighting with a 1–1–1 record.

A few nights later, we stopped in a dry field in the valley blocking access into the rocket belt from those mountains coming from Laos. We were the blocking force, and other units were pushing the NVA toward us. They drove the cattle to us, and we corralled them. They would arrive; we just didn't know when.

The company was spread out on one end of this large multiunit operation. Our perimeter was long, and listening posts were far apart. We were situated in the open area just a little bit from the large, long tree line and forest to our north and west.

There were a few of us together in the tall weeds near the tree line, and we had set up our two-man poncho tents. We created another makeshift mortar pit and dug our fighting/listening hole, which was only slightly closer to the tree line than our sleeping quarters. We rotated turns in the listening hole during the night with our standard two-hour watches.

I was in the hole for my two-hour shift. I thought I heard noises in the tree line. It could be my imagination. It did sound, however, like an occasional clinking of metal. Could I also be hearing whispering? It could be wind in the trees or possibly an animal. It could be my imagination. There was no moon tonight, only the pitch-black of the forest. The dry field around was somewhat lit up by the stars, and I could see the poncho tents, the gear lying around, and the mortar pit a few feet beyond.

That was reassuring, but looking into the forest blackness was scary. Thinking I was hearing sounds was also a little bit nerve-racking. But there was no clear-cut sound or movement to be detected. I sat and waited to see if it was real or imagined, blood pressure and heart rate elevated.

My time in the hole finally ended. Hawthorne came over in a crouched-over walk and jumped into the hole with me. I whispered that I thought I might have heard noises from the tree line. I might have heard whispering and maybe metal clinking. Or maybe it was my imagination or the wind. I crawled out of the hole and headed back to my poncho, where I laid my head down on my backpack.

Bam! There was a loud explosion in the listening hole. Hawthorne was already out of the hole, on the ground, moaning in pain, and trying desperately to keep from screaming. He was in the process of jumping out of the hole and had almost made it when the grenade exploded. It caught his lower legs, but once he heard it landing beside him in the hole, he managed to get the rest of him out before it went off.

They had tossed it in from the tree line or had crawled up closer and tossed it in. They knew we were there, and now they had discovered the trap. They must have moved on through the forest to probe for another exit point because it was quiet for the rest of the night. Hawthorne was medevacked the next day. I haven't seen him since. I can't remember who became the next ammo humper.

★★★

One night we had the opportunity to see "Puff the Magic Dragon." No, it was not the mythical fire-breathing dragon of old but was the real-life current-day equivalent that rained fire down upon the enemy. The enemy called them dragon ships. The Douglas AC-47D was described as "just fucking scary" by those who had seen them. I saw and heard it. It was most awesome.

Puff could fire eighteen thousand rounds per minute with its three mini Gatling guns. Tracer rounds were placed in a gun belt every seven or ten rounds apart. When seen from the ground, all I could see was a constant stream of red spiraling like a corkscrew down to the ground. The plane could blanket every square foot of a football field in sixty seconds and stay aloft for hours, patrolling and protecting US troops, which, of course, was its main task, thus the affectionate nickname from US soldiers.

Using the call sign "Spooky," the gunship could quickly devastate enemy assaults, demolish hill encampments and bunkers, or pulverize ground targets. They could send murderous fire to prepare helicopter landing zones or clear obstacles for jet fighter attacks. Nothing could withstand a full barrage. It could protect us out in the bush and it was astounding to watch.

Miniguns were stuck out the left side of the aircraft, protruding from windows and the cargo doorway. The pilot looked through a sight on his left side window, and when he went into a left turn and bank, he could look down and hurtle constant fire onto enemy troops. It was lethal. It was beautiful. But then again, Puff was on my side. I will always salute "Puff" and their crews.

We had been out here on Mameluke Thrust now for several days. On one of these days, we stopped at the base of a range of small hills. On the ridgetop of the hills, one hill in particular had several tall palm trees, looking to me like the Queen Palms I remembered from California boot camp at MCRD in San Diego.

We set up, and I had some time before dark. It was seemingly not going to rain, but the winds were blowing strong and gusting at ten to twenty knots. The sun was low and would be setting soon. I sat there eating some C rations crap, but I was more involved in watching a particularly interesting set of three palms at the top of the hill that rose above us.

There in the middle, taller than the others and apparently the queen among the queens, was a magnificent tree with fronds spread out in all directions. All three queens were waving and pointing, fronds flowing in the wind. They were making a scene, showing off their power and their majesty. Surveying their domain, they were saying, "We are the sovereigns here over all this land, all that you can see. This is our realm."

Waving about in the winds, showing their authority and dominance, the trees shimmered, sparkled, and glowed brilliantly in the late afternoon sunlight. It was as if they were made of gold and silver leaf tinsel. The sunlight reflected arrows of the brightest colors down to me below. They had the richest flowing, glowing, and shimmering appearance that I had ever seen that was natural and not synthetic. They waved wildly and freely in the strong winds, collecting and reflecting the blazing sun.

I believe that they were instructing us that *this* was their domain and to leave it alone. They were strongly commanding us to get out of there, to leave them alone, and not to harm any more of their home. Those trees were talking to us. If only we could hear. I heard, but leadership would not.

We continued our sweeps, searches, and destruction. Most of the sweeping was through the valley. It was mostly flat fields cut into individual rice paddies surrounded by rice paddy dikes as a means to keep water in the paddy. We tended to walk on those dikes, spread out every ten to fifteen yards or so between marines, hoping to keep boots and socks dry. Rice paddy areas were broken up by small gorges, thin tree lines in the terrain seemingly making it just too difficult to plow into flat paddies by their water buffalo. Those small gorges and thin tree lines made excellent hidden ambush points for the VC and NVA.

It wasn't all flat. There were small rolling hills in the area. Coming down one of those hills in an open area, we approached a tree line farther down. Two VC popped up out from a trapdoor tunnel and blasted our point. They immediately dropped down back into their hole in the ground and took off.

We secured the area, looking for other trapdoors into the ground. A marine "tunnel rat" grabbed a flashlight and a .45 and went down into the tunnel to force the other rats out. It took a while, but he later emerged saying that they wouldn't be bothering us again. He had my complete respect. That was something I don't think I could do. Fortunately, I was never asked.

This encounter did lead to one of the prettiest sights I had ever seen in Vietnam. It had rained. It rained some almost every day. Then usually the skies cleared and the sun would warm everything to a scalding hot, until you were forced once again to pray for rain, which usually came like clockwork about sunset.

After the tunnel incident, we stopped for a while. The sky had cleared, but there was still a lot of moisture and humidity in the air. As I watched the two marines standing over the trapdoor to the tunnel, I saw a full rainbow form out past them, arching into the mountains at the other end of the valley. I grabbed my Instamatic and snapped a few pictures for *National Geographic* (or at least for my own collection).

We had been out here on operation for a few weeks. The word was passed down to us blue-collar folks that we were ending this operation and we'd be helicoptered out of here and back to An Hoa, a few miles away. An Hoa was a Vietnamese village with a big marine air base now built there. It was a good base for staging our operations. It had an enlisted men's club, showers, mail, cots, and hot food. I couldn't wait.

But first we had to get out of here. It seems that Kilo 3/5 drew the short straw. We would be providing security for all the other units as they loaded up their choppers and got out first. We would be the last to go. And it would be Third Platoon and "Basteen" being the last of the last.

That meant that we sat in a dry rice paddy with our backs to a dike and a tree line behind us, watching the tree line in front of us for signs of the bad guys. We were locked and loaded, ready for trouble, but none came while we waited. The others left.

The day passed painstakingly slowly, and I was envious of all these guys getting back to An Hoa before me. Finally, after baking in the sun for nearly another full day, we were next to go. It turned out that I was on the very last chopper to load up and leave. Twelve or thirteen of us were the last ones at the dike in front of the tree line. We had been there all day. We loaded into the back end of a Chinook helicopter right there in the dry rice paddy.

A Chinook is a top-mounted two-engine helicopter with one engine in the front and one in the back. The rear gate could be lowered or raised to allow loading of troops or cargo. They also had the ability to sling cargo nets below them, which increased capacity. They were the workhorse in Vietnam.

I was thankful to be leaving this place. It had been quiet today, but being the last to leave had given us the feeling that the bad guys were just waiting for the protection to be leaving and not having any protection for themselves. I sat on the canvas bench along the inside of the helicopter and looked out the opposite window to where I had been sitting against the dike two or three minutes ago.

Bam! A poof of black smoke and dirt exploded into the air exactly where I had just been sitting against the dike. It seemed to have been an RPG (rocket-propelled grenade) aimed at our helicopter. I did not hear the explosion because the engines were at full power as we tried to take off and get out of there. I saw two or three more explosions on the dike we'd just left. I was thinking, *Please don't hit this helicopter.*

We lifted off and immediately turned away from that far tree line. We barely cleared the trees at the near end, where we had just spent the day sunbathing. We made it unscathed and would soon land at An Hoa. As far as I was concerned, I was calling this another close call. I added it to my list.

Ron "Pack Rat" Heath. This must have been a day patrol because he did not have his enormous backpack with him today.

The two marines were standing over the trapdoor to the tunnel, waiting for our tunnel rat to come back out.

In the air, the sky had cleared and a rainbow had formed due to the humidity remaining after the showers.

This was a two-man poncho tent situated next to a listening/fighting hole out on Operation Mameluke Thrust. Behind me were our poncho tent, mortar pit, and the listening/fighting hole where Hawthorne was hit by the grenade.

Some of the fields and rice paddies were enormous on Operation Mameluke Thrust. Unfortunately, they didn't offer a lot of protection if we received incoming.

On sweep during Operation Mameluke Thrust, spread out walking the dikes. There were plenty of ridges, dips, and tree lines for hit-and-run attacks.

Harold ("HE"—high explosive) Bakken was preparing his poncho tent for the evening rains. We were parked right up against the forest, which allowed stealth attacks by Charlie.

CHAPTER 14

OPERATION MEADE RIVER

It was now late November 1968. We arrived back at An Hoa via air coach delivery, and we were given our choice of mail, beer, mess hall, or showers. Mobeck and I chose showers, opting to avoid the rush for beer. He said, "Race ya," and off we went, running down the hill to the enlisted men's outdoor showers like kids at a water park.

Concerning showers in Vietnam, there was good news and bad news. The bad news was that once the thrill of the once-a-month cleansing and cooling shower was over and once you had toweled off all new and squeaky clean, that left you completely unprotected and at the mercy of the elements. The elements, in this case, were things like mosquitos, gnats, flies, ants, and the sun.

Without the protection of all that sweat, mud, crud, body odor, and accumulated bug splatter, your body was a waiting feast for all the creepy-crawlies and flying insects in the district. You were a neon sign attracting anything and everything that bit, stuck, probed, or injected. Without that gunk, marines fried bright pink in the Vietnam sun.

Normally it took about three days of heavy-duty sweating and sleeping on the ground to rebuild that important protective body armor. I was almost to the point where I didn't want to take a shower; it wasn't worth the agony afterward to rebuild the protection.

In reality, however, the good news about showers was that they made suffering the bad news worthwhile. The good news about showers was that they felt so good. After all, just remember how luxurious it is to be able to clean the crud out from between your toes and to discover, once again, that your hair is actually made up of individual strands rather than just one piece of matted-down straw. Remember how it feels to lather up, thick with soap, and to rinse off with cool, clean water. It was so nice. I promised myself that when I was back in the real world, I would take a shower every day forever.

★★★

Every once in a while, you come across somebody you know who was a soul mate or a friend from a previous life. Mobeck was that guy to us. From the first time you met him, you knew you liked him.

He was one of those people who always had some type of smile on his face—maybe a sly, wry smile, or maybe a broad, happy grin, or sometimes that fake "Oh, I am so surprised" grin—but when you were around him, you were probably laughing about something.

Mobeck was one of those naturally enthusiastic guys who didn't care what he was doing; it would be at full speed ahead, and he was happy to do it. He was the only guy I ever knew who wanted to race while digging a trench with E-tools! I have a picture of him and another guy smiling and laughing at themselves while they were covered with calamine lotion in order to fight off a chigger infestation.

We were the first ones to the showers. In fact, we were the only ones at the showers. They weren't much—just a big square piece of cement, four wooden crate walls around it, with an opening on one wall serving as the door (no roof or ceiling), and eight or ten water pipes about six feet tall with showerheads on them. The water pipes had round handled shutoff valves on each, allowing the water to flow or be shut off. There were no hot water valves; the water temp was whatever the water temp was.

But it was nice running water, cool and clean. We started luxuriating and lathering up, saying, "Ooooh" and "Aaaahh" and "Oh, that's good." We were indeed kings at the moment.

I finally had had enough and started thinking about getting a beer. I didn't want to miss out on this priority. I would not be happy if the club ran out of beer just before I got there. I rinsed off and started toweling dry. Mobeck, though, being enthusiastic and enjoying everything he did, said to me, "Watch this; I'll lather up so that I look like Frosty the Snowman."

He got completely lathered from head to toe. No part of his body was showing through the soap except his eyes. Just then, the water stopped. Mobeck stood in silent disbelief. "Huh?" he finally said.

I was smiling. "What just happened?"

Then he yelled out at the top of his lungs, "Hey, where's my water?"

Somebody came down the hill to our lowly platform and said, "Oh, the officers are having their showers now. The water will be back on in about a half hour."

Standing under the sun in about one-hundred-plus-degree heat, it didn't take long for all that soap to bake and cake. Within a few minutes, he looked more like "Plaster of Paris" man than Frosty the Snowman.

I laughed so hard that my sides hurt. I had tears in my eyes. I couldn't see. I chuckled to Mobeck, "I'll see you later; I'm gonna go have a beer." I left Mobeck standing under the hot sun looking like a plaster of paris statue fuming with rage.

Much later, after they had reinstated the water and he had rinsed off, he found us at the enlisted club. I said to him, "Hey, I've known you for six or eight months now, but I don't even know your first name. Everybody calls you Mobeck. What's your first name?"

"Sparky."

I burst out laughing because it was so perfect—"happy-go-lucky Sparky Mobeck." That just fit perfectly.

After getting out of the service (we got out on the same day), I decided to drive around the country seeing the sights. "Sparky" (Don Mobeck was his real name) joined me on the cross-country odyssey. We traveled across most of the country, living off friends and relatives, playing golf, meeting girls, visiting friends from Nam, and seeing the sights. It was all good fun. I'll never give up those memories.

Years later, at one of the reunions, I found out he had died in a car accident (probably going 150 miles per hour).

★★★

The An Hoa military base and airfield was a sprawling compound capable of holding a lot of marines and other military personnel, equipment, weapons and ammunition. It had a mess hall, showers with running water (although outdoors), a head with toilets where you could sit rather than squat, buildings and tents with cots for sleeping under a roof rather than under the stars, and an enlisted men's club where I wouldn't be drinking well water from a rice paddy. What more in the world could anybody possibly want?

It was also a good place for regrouping, reorganizing, resupply, and recovery. It was used as a starting place for major operations, and we usually got helicopter air service to the new operation rather than being forced to walk in.

We arrived last in from our part in Operation Mameluke Thrust to find that there was no more room inside the base for us, no accommodations. We would get cots, but they would not be in any of the actual buildings or tents. They would be outside the base, under the stars. Nevertheless, I was happy; I would not be sleeping on the ground. I had a poncho that I could drape over myself, so even in the unlikely event that it rained (ha!), I should be fine.

The first night back, after a nice cleansing shower, a hot meal of real food, clean clothes, and drinks at the EM club, I slept like a baby. It didn't rain, and I wouldn't have noticed if it had. The next day, we ate real food again, cleaned weapons, and sat around outside on our cots telling lies to each other about home, girls, food, hobbies … whatever. We busied ourselves by decorating helmets with pictures of the Grim Reaper and saying things like, "Get some" (the 3/5 motto) and other inane things.

Night came, and this time we repeated dinner and the EM club only. I had had a shower yesterday. Didn't need that. I'd read my mail today. Didn't need that. After the EM club, I found my way out to my cot with only a little difficulty. I reclined on the cot and pulled the poncho over me like a blanket. It felt so good to be able to stretch out on a nice smooth long canvas cot without rocks or branches sticking me and without snakes and large insects crawling across my body. I especially liked knowing I wouldn't wake up in a river of rainwater and mud.

However, tonight it rained. I wasn't worried; I had a poncho.

Tonight, though, I learned another truth about the Marine Corps: I learned that a USMC-issue cot was about two inches longer than a USMC-issue poncho. Therefore, no matter how you arranged it, there were about two inches of cot that would collect rainwater while you were sleeping in it. And the rainwater would pool in the low parts of the canvas. It kept you in a cold bath all night long. I never knew that before about cots and ponchos.

A few days passed. We were prepped for another operation, this time called "Meade River." We would lift off in a massive wave of CH-46 Chinooks, with about twelve to thirteen marines aboard each, plus two pilots. It was November 20, 1968. We'd be leaving as soon as the fog lifted and pilots could see to land in the bush. We were going back to Dodge City, and then we'd be sweeping it clear. After that, we would be climbing through the nearby hills and into the mountains to interrupt the NVA supply train of men, equipment, and supplies into our TAOR (tactical area of responsibility) around Da Nang.

In the meantime, we sat at the An Hoa Air Base, waiting for the clouds to lift. We were spread out along the entire taxiway, lounging about and telling lies as if we had good sense. I was waiting near the chopper I thought I'd be assigned to. Captain Meyers wandered by, checking to see that we were ready—or at least appeared to be ready. I had my Instamatic camera handy, so I asked him if I could get a picture.

He was pleased and posed with his radio handset. I got a great picture of him set against a background of low clouds with fog beginning to lift and of troops waiting for good flying weather. The captain appeared happy and confident. He was a short-timer, so this would be his last operation.

Later, the clouds lifted sufficiently for takeoff and insertion into our first stop on Meade River. I joined the squad that was getting on this chopper. I was last in line. (Somehow, I have made a career of being *last*—last in line, last to know.) I snapped a picture of the other marines boarding the aircraft. They were giving the "office grunt" their dog tag information as they boarded.

I was moving up, getting close. Captain Meyers came over to me and said, "Basteen, we're only taking thirteen on this helicopter. I want you to go down over there and get on that helicopter with Third Platoon. I'll be taking your place."

"Yes, sir."

I walked down to the helicopter he mentioned and got on board with Third Platoon. We were finally ready for liftoff. Just as I was sitting down on the canvas bench, there was still one last marine climbing up the rear ramp. Even before the kid had gotten all the way into the helicopter, the pilot lifted the front end up and we started our climb out.

That last marine hadn't quite gotten in yet, and as we tilted up into our climb, he lost his balance and tumbled out of the helicopter backward to the ramp, ass over teakettle. He did a one and a half gainer, landing smack on his backpack on the steel runway below. I was sure he had broken his back. We couldn't do anything about it, and the pilots didn't even know anything about it. Off we went.

We flew for only ten or fifteen minutes to our insertion point. As we approached to land, we found that some of the landing zones were hot and the helicopters were taking incoming. Nasty. I didn't like this. However, we landed. Jumping off the helicopter in the open field, I ran as fast as I could while carrying that heavy mortar and baseplate. We all made it to the tree line for cover. Then we began to regroup into recognizable units once again.

It was later, after we had regrouped and reorganized, that I heard that the helicopter carrying Captain Meyers had been shot down and crashed on landing. There were five KIAs. Apparently, both pilots had been shot as they made the landing approach.

The crash killed pilots Captain William Emerson, Lieutenant John R. Harrell, and three Kilo infantrymen: Captain David W. Myers, Lance Corporal Donald W. McBride, and Private First Class William P. Smith Jr. The crew chief and flight engineer on the flight were thrown clear in the crash but were seriously injured. One suffered a critical head injury and the other a ruptured spleen. The other Kilo members survived. Lyndon Wilson was aboard and was one who survived. Captain Meyers did not.

Wow, I was thinking how Captain Meyers had taken my place. I was meant to be on that chopper. Of course, nobody could have known beforehand what would happen. It could have been any chopper. Happenstance had played its fickle hand once again. Today it was on my side. This was definitely going in my close calls list. Once again, as so many times before, I was sorry for Captain Meyers and the others but happy that it wasn't me. I realized that only being close is not always so bad.

Captain Meyers represented so many others in this stupid war—coming from a family of loved ones and friends; a history of doing things and accomplishments; plans and hopes for the future. He just needed to get past the hurdle of this war, like so many others.

I only scratched at my C rations in the high grasses as I dwelled on it. Do we call that luck, chance, happenstance, or God's intervention? How many close calls had I had? How many did I get? I figured that I must be getting close to the end. You only get so many, right?

Out there in the Nam, there was nobody more deserving than anyone else for safe passage through a tour, and there was nobody who deserved to receive the punishment this place could give out over anyone else. Personal outcomes seemed to be random, arbitrary, and unknowable. The rewards for safe passage were continued life and opportunity for love, family, and career. Receiving what this place could dish out meant continuing pain and anguish for families and friends, with thoughts forever of what might have been.

Many years later, the following note was written to Captain Meyers by his niece. It was a nice tribute to a missing uncle, and I submit it here as a tribute to all those who have fallen, including Captain David Meyers. It illustrates the universal feeling of grief from loved ones, even years later, to those who are now gone from us forever:

> February 21, 2005
>
> You are my uncle, my mom's little brother. You are missed beyond words. What happened that awful day in November 1968? You were only three days shy of finishing your tour.

The phone call, the telegram that Mom received, the tears that Grandma refused to show at your funeral ... Your children and your wife were so lost without you.

We are all adults now, with our own families, yet our children will never hear their uncle Dave's voice, know the sound of his laughter, or know the love that you were capable of giving. We miss you, especially Mom.

From your niece,

Melissa

Captain David Wendell Myers: K CO. Third Battalion, Fifth Marines, First Marine Division

Purple Heart, National Defense, Vietnam service, Vietnam campaign, Ames, Iowa: July 7, 1938–November 20, 1968

Panel 38W, line 019

★★★

We continued the operation, sweeping and clearing the area. We'd been here before, and I was sure other marines would be here again. On one of the resupply runs, when the helicopter landed and they started off-loading C rations, ammunition, and water, the kid who fell out of the helicopter at the start of all this got off and wandered over to our hole. He sat down as if nothing had happened and as if he had good sense.

I looked at him and said, "I thought you fell out of our helicopter and broke your back."

He said, "Yeah, it did hurt a little for a day or so, but it's okay."

Somebody piped up, "You *dumb shit*. If you had complained enough, you'd probably have received a golden parachute ticket home."

He said, "Oh, I didn't think of that."

I thought to myself that maybe I wasn't the dumbest one out here after all.

The next day, we started our climb into the mountains. The way up was steep, and we were all sweating like indentured servants in a sweatshop (actually, we were indentured servants in a sweatshop). I stopped and turned around to get a few pictures, and I could see An Hoa off in the distance. It was a tough climb into the mountains, but after a while, we made it, unobstructed and unhindered.

For the next few days, we followed the trails in and among the beautiful forests and lush vegetation. We saw mountain streams and waterfalls. The sunlight filtered down through the trees and managed to brighten up some areas while throwing shadows in others, making every step a walk into another work of art. Only the exotic birdcalls and the monkeys paralleling our course broke the stillness and quiet of the woods. The monkeys were still throwing rocks at us. I was enjoying the hike. I noticed that in the forest, it didn't seem so hot anymore.

One morning as we pushed on, I was back somewhere in the middle of the caravan. We had been walking on a well-worn trail through the woods. The stillness was suddenly broken by an M16 on full automatic up ahead, about where I would expect point to be. We stopped for a few moments, and I wondered if we should get down. Who was doing the shooting? What was going on?

Then, without a word, we pressed on. After a minute or two, I came to a bend in the trail that had a small footbridge across one of the many mountain streams we'd seen. This was, of course, a major trail coming from Laos, used frequently by the NVA. I discovered what the shooting was about.

There in the stream lay a dead NVA soldier with the top of his head neatly severed just above the eyes. I would have liked to stop and examine that head, as it looked as if it had been opened up surgically for autopsy. It looked just like the pictures. But we keep moving.

I had no idea why there was only one NVA out here alone. Maybe his buddies ran off. We pressed on, looking for more bad guys, their caves and tunnels, their hospitals in the ground, their supply camps, and whatever else we could find. We stopped at night, wherever we happened to be.

The idea was to resupply us every two days. We should get fresh water, fresh ammo, and fresh C rations every other day via helicopter. Unfortunately, it didn't always work out that way, especially in the mountains, where low clouds could sit on the ground as fog for days.

We had been up here in the mountains southwest of An Hoa for several days already. The purpose was to close down the trails into the Da Nang area and deny Charlie access so he couldn't set up and launch rockets into the city.

The high country had been beautiful—tall rain forest trees, thick vegetation, running streams, and waterfalls. However, there were also lots of insects and things that thrived in the heat and humidity. Today temperature and the dew point met. The fog set in. It was so thick that we didn't even do our patrols or ambushes. We just sat. We sat for several days.

The first day wasn't too bad; we still had food. By the next day, we had run out of C rations and were beginning to get hungry. The next day was worse, and after that, it was terrible. I remember sitting on a fallen tree with four or five other guys, just talking. We looked like starving birds on a telephone line.

One guy said, "I miss Mom's pork chops and eggs."

Another said, "Grandma makes the best apple pie."

We were all drooling and hungry. Talking about it made it worse. Then a skinny kid from the Old South down at the end of the log, said, "I know what we can do—we'll make soup."

"Huh?"

"Yeah, we'll go pick some roots and boil them and make a tasty soup, just like at home." He jumped up, went over to some leafy-looking plant, and pulled it up. Sure enough, there was some white tuber-looking bulb thing at the end of it. He said, "Go find some of these."

We all jumped up and went to find roots. We shook the dirt off them and dumped them all into the kid's helmet. He had taken the helmet liner out of it, so we had our pot.

We used our canteens to fill the helmet with water, and then we all submitted the last of our heat tabs to heat it. We built a makeshift "stove" out of rocks and started boiling our soup. A few minutes later, the last of the heat tabs had burned down, so it was time to taste our soup. I'm sure the water never boiled. In fact, I'm sure it hardly got warm.

It was the most god-awful bitterest-tasting thing I'd ever tasted. It was probably poisonous too. Everybody spit it out—even the kid from the South. To show our appreciation to the kid for using up all our heat tabs, most of our fresh water, and making us wait in anticipation for "bitter-root soup," we beat the snot out of him. Everybody took a turn.

Finally, the weather cleared and the choppers began to fly. We were resupplied, and I got my four C rations meals. I immediately gobbled two of them. I don't remember heating either of them. Even the glutamate tasted good.

Steve Cronen came over to me after feasting on his C rations and told me that he had been told to pack up; he was going home. He was to jump on the next chopper up there and head back to An Hoa. It was early December 1968, maybe December 2.

"Well, you damn son of a bitch," I said. "You're gonna leave all these good times here and go home?"

Cronen laughed that big hearty laugh and said "Yup. I'll see you back there." He was grinning from ear to ear. A little while later, one of the ugly helicopters arrived with more supplies. It was one of those with red gills and looked like a grasshopper or locust. As soon as they off-loaded the supplies, Cronen turned his back and ran to get on board. He never looked back; he never waved. He almost dove into the side door. Cronen reminded me of my dog at home doing the happy dance when I asked him if he wanted to go for a walk. It was pure happiness. No kid sitting on Santa Claus's knee was ever this happy.

The next day, it was back to the ol' grind and we were back to sweeping again. From my early childhood days, at night I was one of those guys who couldn't sleep on my back because my nose plugged up. So I'd lie on one side until a nostril plugged up, and then I rolled over to the other side until that nostril plugged up. I'd been doing this since my first night in Nam, always making some noise. But on one of these nights as I did it, I realized that I was only waking halfway up and consciously rolling over slowly and quietly, not rustling a leaf or a blade of grass. Then I'd go fully back to sleep.

In the morning, I remembered realizing what I had done, and I congratulated myself on beginning to have finally acclimated to Vietnam and nature here. I could now sleep in dry vegetation, wake up and roll over without making any noise, and then go fully back to sleep. Better yet, I seemed to be getting more good-quality deep sleep in the time that I had available for it. It was if I was sleeping but my mind was alert and aware. I was quite pleased with myself. I was building confidence that I could actually handle this. I didn't know how long I had been doing it, but it had been for a while.

On operation, we usually hunkered down at night and then got moving again a little after dawn. I had been in this rhythm for some time. I had been able, naturally and without anyone waking me, to wake up just after first light when the sky became a silver gray in the west as the night faded away and a yellow-orange in the east just before the sun actually rose over the horizon. I had been able to do this for several months now. I never really thought too much about it. It had become natural.

One early morning, though, I realized that I was now waking up before first light. The sky was still black and the stars were still out, but I could see just a sliver of a silver-blue streak rising in the east, splitting the blackness. It was the very first light. I woke and sat up, fully awake, ready to go. I didn't need all that sleep anymore. Was I actually getting used to this? I thought that maybe I was.

On one of these mornings, I had an insight that I would never have believed. I made (what was for me) a major discovery. I woke and sat up, as was habit now, and studied the silver-blue sky in the east just beginning to push back the black night and stars. Enjoying the stillness and the view, I was surrounded by trees and branches, leaves and tall grasses, weeds all around. There wasn't a breath of wind. It was as still and quiet as could be. There wasn't even the sound of any insects. Nothing was moving. It was a dead calm and I realized that I was actually enjoying this morning stillness.

Then suddenly everything shook. It was as if a sonic boom had passed by, but it was a soundless sonic boom. It was quick and quiet. Everything shook. It passed over and through us and then was over and gone in a millisecond. Every leaf on every tree and every weed and every blade of grass in sight shook or bounced all at once. It was a tiny shake and bounce. It was almost imperceptible. It happened all at once, and it happened only once. But it happened.

I wondered about that and about what it was, but I couldn't figure it out. Everything was just as still as before. I even wondered if it had really happened. Then I forgot about it as we got busy doing other things.

However, a few days later, it happened again. I woke up just as the first streak of light was beginning to push back the night. It was still as could be—no wind, no breeze, no noise, no movement—and I sat watching the sky becoming day, watching the stars fade away one by one. All of a sudden, *poof!* Everything shook and bounced. Everything moved ever so slightly. It moved only once, and only a little, just like before. Then it was gone.

I puzzled about this for some time. Finally, my explanation—and I have no idea if it is true or not—is that there is a shock wave that travels around the earth just in front of the rising sun. The sun appears to us to be traveling around the earth, and it lights the area in front of it as it travels. A moving line around the earth divides the day from the night, or night from the day. The line of light "pushes" the air in front of it (just a little), and that creates a shock wave in front of the rising sun, just as a boat traveling in water makes a wave in front of it as it cuts through the water.

The shock wave was not large. In fact, it was very small, but it was just enough to move a leaf slightly on a still night as it raced around the world. At the equator, that line would be moving about eleven hundred miles per hour. I know that it exists; I saw it twice.

★★★

On one of our helicopter resupply drops, we also received two new grunts. They got off the chopper wide-eyed and scared, brand-new FNGs fresh from the States. They had only been in the country a few days and were flown out to join us. They didn't even have any time to acclimate to the new situation as I did at the old 3/5 Battalion area. They were suddenly out in the bush.

After welcoming them to Kilo, whoever was making duty rosters said that they were to go out on the listening post tonight (Welcome to the Nam!). I saw their panicked eyes, the tight lips, and that "Oh shit" look on their faces. I almost laughed, but that would have been cruel. They were scared—and rightly so. They had *no* idea what to expect or what to do.

I have no idea what came over me, but I had been feeling pretty good lately and hadn't been out on one of these for some time. I volunteered to take one of their places. "I'll go out tonight," I said.

What in the world was I thinking? I couldn't believe I'd said that. It turned out that neither of the FNGs went out that night. I think Haycraft went out with me. He also volunteered.

On watch at the listening post, I thought about my rash spur-of-the moment decision. I wondered if I was being a good guy or if I was just being stupid. I was getting to be a short-timer, and I should be more conservative. You didn't want to get killed or wounded after spending nearly thirteen months being miserable and now almost ready to go home. The idea was that if you're gonna get killed or wounded in the Nam, then do it early in your tour so you don't spend a year being miserable and then killed or wounded. I now had more than a year invested.

Was I getting a short-timer's attitude and being cocky or was I just feeling more comfortable with all this now? Only time would tell. However, I just couldn't see putting two brand-new FNGs out on listening post on their very first night in the bush. At first light, Haycraft and I got up and headed back. No contact, no sweat.

I felt good about doing it. I felt no regret about volunteering to go out. Actually, I wasn't even worried. But I kept wondering if this was being stupid, like standing up in a firefight. Or was I actually concerned for fellow marines? I had been warned about that way back in boot camp. Even so, I felt that I *could* and should do it. I *could* handle it. It was right.

After Operation Mameluke Thrust, An Hoa filled up, and being the last to arrive, we got cots but had to sleep outside under the stars. We busied ourselves shooting the shit, playing cards, and decorating helmets.

Outside An Hoa, I learned that a USMC-issue cot was about two inches longer than a USMC-issue poncho. It would catch every raindrop and collect it in a pool at the low spot in the canvas. I never knew that before.

MGM didn't look particularly happy right then. He'd probably learned about the size of cots and ponchos last night too.

Bastien standing by the helicopter he was scheduled to take into Operation Meade River. Low clouds and fog delayed takeoff for several hours and eliminated any element of surprise.

The clouds finally lifted, and we loaded up for our flight into Dodge City and Operation Meade River. I was last in line to board. Captain Meyers came over and told me to go down and get on the Third Platoon chopper. He would take my place on this one.

Sadly, this chopper was shot down during insertion and five were killed.

Captain Meyers shortly before the clouds and fog lifted, allowing us to depart for Operation Meade River. He looked confident and happy. He was a short-timer and was probably looking forward to his last operation.

In the mountains southwest of An Hoa, the low clouds and fog moved in for several days. Here we sat, waiting for resupply, telling stories and lies about food and home cooking by Mom, Grandma, girlfriends, wives … anything.

That only made the hunger worse.

Haycraft and Doc McKillip wait along with other grunts for resupply. It appears that Doc was being requested to be somewhere else.

Haycraft and some guys whose names I should remember, but it has been over fifty years, so those are gone.

Nothing to do but wait for resupply. We were not even running patrols.

It looks no different than three guys standing around on the corner back home, wasting time after school or work.

Steve Cronen making his big escape off the mountain and back to the real world. He never looked back, never waved. He was grinning from ear to ear last I saw him. We did meet up again in Minneapolis after I got home.

CHAPTER 15

GOING HOME

We mucked about for a couple more days, and then we got the word that we were going back to An Hoa. Nothing was happening in the mountains. The brass weren't getting their quota of kills. We all wanted hot food, showers, and beer. Therefore, we came down out of the hills. It was much easier and faster coming down the mountain than it was climbing up the mountain, but still, the trek was long, hot, and tiring. On the way down to An Hoa, on the last leg, we walked alongside a tranquil river that meandered right on past the base.

It so invited and tempted us to jump in and go swimming that after we found cots and dropped gear once back at the base, we did exactly that. The slow-moving river wound between hills and ridges and had wide, flat green banks of good grazing lands. The jungle forest was pushed back a good distance. Several of us rushed to the cool river waters, much better than showers on a cement slab. This was a nice end to another long stretch in the bush. Everyone had fun splashing like kids. Overall, this stretch wasn't too bad.

Back in the base (we were inside the base this time), I was told to go to the company office. Once there, I was told to go to the armory and turn in my M16. I'd be going home tomorrow! Somebody else in the platoon was already carrying my mortar. I was happy for the news but not overly excited. I had been expecting it to happen any day, as it was already about December 18 or 19. My thirteen months were nearly up. I only had a week or two at most left anyway. I turned in my weapon, but now I felt naked and vulnerable. I packed what little I had into my smallish backpack and thought that I'd be reunited with my seabag and personal items somewhere on the way home, maybe in Da Nang or Okinawa. I wasn't concerned. I would go home dressed as is, if that's what it took.

Trying to sleep that night, I was actually uncomfortable in the cot. I wasn't really asleep, simply pretending to be with eyes closed, probably thinking about getting home. Was it possible that I was not comfortable because I wasn't on the ground? Or was I worried because I didn't have a weapon?

Then the explosions started. I heard someone yell "Incoming!" and small arms fire. Guys were running out to their defensive positions. They had weapons and assigned places. I had no weapons and no assigned place to go. What the heck? Now what was I to do? So I sat up and waited. If they got this far, I was going hand to hand. I felt naked, helpless, and vulnerable. However, they didn't get that far. It was just another small harassment, a few mortar rounds and some small arms incoming, and then they disappeared back into the hills or the jungle.

Morning arrived and I got a nice hot real breakfast while sitting at a table using silverware. The silverware was not really silver, but it was metal and now included a fork and knife. I laughed, wondering if I could remember what I used each of those for. I don't remember what I had to eat. It didn't matter because it was hot, real, and tasty. I don't remember if I gobbled it so fast because it was hot, because it was real, or because it was so tasty. Maybe I gobbled it so fast because in my thirteen months, I had learned that you could be attacked at anytime and anywhere and you best not be sitting there fat, dumb, and happy.

Sometime later that morning I got on a Chinook CH-46 helicopter with one other marine whom I did not know, a crew chief, and two pilots. We were going to Da Nang and then I was going home! We lifted off, gained some altitude, and headed back … right over Arizona Territory, Dodge City, and the Go Noi Island area where we had done Operations Allen Brook, Mameluke Thrust, and Meade River.

I recognized some of the landmarks, so I knew where I was as I looked out the window on the other side of the cabin. I thought that I saw the same rice paddy dike and tree line where we sat all day as security for the rest of the battalion as they returned to An Hoa at the end of Mameluke Trust. All of a sudden, *bam!* The window shattered into a hundred little pieces, floated around in the cabin for a moment, and then flew out the back end of the helicopter.

I was stunned. What the heck was that? All I could think was that we had been shot. The crew chief ran over and started investigating and examining the rear engine. I noticed that we were starting down. I thought, *Oh shit. I don't even have a weapon.*

However, the engine seemed okay, and the crew chief went back to his normal position. He couldn't tell us what happened because the noise was so loud; the words would stream out the back end of the chopper just as the window had. The helicopter leveled off just above the ground, and we were racing past water buffalo, farmers, and huts at about one hundred miles per hour. We got to a tree line, and the pilot had to climb to get over the trees. On the other side, he descended to within a few feet of the ground. I was convinced that we were crashing and he was having fun hot-rodding in this expensive military machine … with *me* on board.

We finally got to Da Nang, as evidenced by the large number of buildings. We climbed to a decent elevation and then slowed down. We landed near the same place where I had arrived so long ago. Somebody took me to the enlisted men's quarters and showed me where the mess hall was. Unfortunately, I would *not* be going home today. That plane was already gone. I'd be on tomorrow's plane. Sit tight. Hurry up and wait.

I didn't have anything to read. I had nothing to do. I went to take a shower. I went to dinner at the mess hall. Finally, night came, and I pretended to sleep, tossing and turning on a cot that I couldn't get comfortable on. What was with these cots all of a sudden? I was grumbling in my head about these uncomfortable cots when suddenly the rockets started inbound. I heard the blasts, down the field a way, fortunately, and then I heard the sirens. People were running to their defensive positions, and they had weapons. I had no weapon and no assigned place to go, so I sat up and waited. If they got this far, I was going hand to hand. However, they didn't get that far. It was just a handful of rockets meant to harass and cause whatever damage they could.

I was awake most of the night, sitting up on the cot. I had finally taken my boots off, and I stared at them sitting on the floor. I noticed the dry leather around the toes with all the polish worn off and the creases and scratches across the top where the shrapnel had tried its best to get me but could only come close. I couldn't even remember the battles where I got those. I noticed the rubber soles, markedly worn down now, and I wondered how many miles we had traveled together. These boots and I had been over a lot of territory, and we had been through some wild events. These boots had become a part of me. They were comfortable, comforting, and friendly. They were my friends. I'd be keeping these boots.

In the morning, I had another "last breakfast." Whatever it was, it was good.

When it was time for boarding, I went over to the terminal. People started coming out of the woodwork. There were marines, army, navy, and air force people all getting in line to board the big, beautiful Continental 707 jet. There were officers, enlisted, and even some civilians. There wasn't a lot of talking. It was as if everyone was a stranger. It seemed that there were not two guys leaving Vietnam from the same unit. I was alone and didn't know anybody else. I smirked as I thought that everybody was afraid to talk because if they did, somebody on the loudspeaker would say, "Sorry, this flight has been canceled. Return to your units."

We loaded up and sat quietly, afraid that anything out of the ordinary would still get the flight canceled. Everybody was polite. We addressed the good-looking flight attendants as "ma'am," said "please" and "thank you," and talked in quiet tones. We were all collectively holding our breath, anticipating a cancellation notice that we sensed was sure to arrive any minute.

We were still quiet and holding our breath as we taxied out. It was as still and quiet as a night on listening watch. Turning left onto runway 18, nobody spoke. The engines spooled up for a southbound departure. We accelerated down the runway. I knew that we'd be climbing out within throwing distance away from Go Noi Island. We weren't out of Nam yet. We needed to turn left and climb out over the ocean as soon as possible.

The nose rose. We lifted off. We were climbing! Nobody breathed. A few seconds longer and it was gear up. The pilot banked left. The cabin erupted in cheers and applause. The cheering and yelling exploded as if the Minnesota Vikings had just won the Super Bowl. It continued until we crossed the beaches and we were out over open water. There were handshakes all around, in addition to laughter, hugs, crying, and a collective sigh of relief. We were leaving Vietnam behind. We had made it.

The meandering river that runs just past the An Hoa military base. Some of the hills and mountains that we humped on my last operation are visible in the background under the clouds.

Cooling off in the river was like a vacation day—laughing, splashing, and feeling good after a long walk down the mountains.

THIRTEEN MONTHS

This is a view from the mountains, looking down into one of the valleys. It looks so pretty and serene. What a shame that we were killing and bombing the heck out of this land.

CHAPTER 16

AFTERMATH

I sit now at my desk and computer, removed from Vietnam by more than fifty years. As mentioned before, it never leaves you entirely. It lives inside, sometimes deeply hidden and sometimes just below the surface, but it is always waiting and wanting to get out. It'll sneak out in fits and spurts through dreams—or it'll burst out all at once by a smell, a sound, or some random sight that triggers the floodgates of memory. In some cases, it just oozes out like oil from the ground in Texas. It shows up as lost and empty feelings for loved ones, anger about anything or everything, and it comes with a need to subdue it using alcohol or drugs—any way possible.

I reflect on my thirteen months there so long ago. Now that I am personally back healthy, whole, and undamaged, I can say that it was a good experience and I'm glad I did it; I just wouldn't want to do it again. It was a learning and a growing experience for me, turning a kid into an adult.

For many others whom I know were there and for the many others I don't know, it was not a good experience and not one to reflect back on. For those I know, even the happy reunions, phone calls, and get-togethers consist of happy laughter and old stories but always some unwanted crying and dark memories as well.

★★★

There's a saying: "Not everyone who lost his life in Vietnam died there. Not everyone who came home from Vietnam ever left there." There are soldiers who came back but never really moved on. They were stuck there, mentally, emotionally, and psychologically. Whether it was due to PTSD from the stress or a desire for the adrenaline rush of the danger and excitement, some were never able to get back to the real world.

Since that time, I have absorbed and watched the changes in society, politics, viewpoints, and behaviors. One day has followed another, and seasons have followed each other, making it seem that things never change on a day-to-day basis. In reality, the world and the country, politics, behaviors, and social norms are always changing. Change has been happening in the country since the Pilgrims landed, but the pace and magnitude of change expanded enormously around the time of the Vietnam War. It was the sixties, a decade of change.

And 1968 was a year of profound change. The United States absorbed the assassinations of Bobby Kennedy and Martin Luther King. There was the Tet Offensive and the My Lai Massacre in Vietnam, and widening anti–Vietnam War sentiment brought the riots that caused President Johnson to decide not to run for reelection. There were riots and bloodshed at the Democratic National Nominating Convention in Chicago. Black athletes imposed the Black Power salute at the Winter Olympics as racial tensions and race riots flared in cities across the land.

Trust in government was recast from a naive and innocent acceptance that what they told us and what they did was in our best interests into a deep, dark skepticism that government was lying to us and only in it for their own personal gain. The public perspective of the military changed from it once being considered "protector/hero" to it being considered imperialist, occupier, and "baby killer."

I processed out of the marines at Camp Pendleton on April 1, 1969. There were so many of us with short times remaining that they decided to save some payroll money and let us out early. There wasn't time to retrain us, and they couldn't send us back to Nam. One morning we woke up, and anybody having a discharge date of earlier than September 30, 1969, would be getting out on April 1, 1969. We all thought it was just another Marine Corps trick (an April Fools' Day trick). However, it wasn't.

While struggling to get back to life and finish college, there was always that open and unanswered discussion I promised to have with myself "sometime" after Vietnam. It would be the discussion about war and morality. Is war moral? Is killing in war moral? What is morality? Should we have even been there? This would be a difficult conversation.

I never truly wanted to revisit it. It simply wouldn't go away. So one night, fueled by the grape, I decided to tackle it. It was a cold winter night back at the U of M in a firetrap apartment near the campus. After much thought and reflection, I came away with some ideas that have at least allowed me to continue on with life.

War has been with us since civilization began because the leaders of a civilization usually found it cheaper and easier to plunder other cities and towns for their wealth than it was to create wealth themselves. Taking resources, land, treasure, and people as slaves originated early on and has been with us ever since. Throughout history, it has been accepted as normal that "might makes right," along with all the other trappings of war, including slavery as an economic engine.

Western countries have had a Reformation and Enlightenment, so many of those ideas should have become discounted and rejected. Unfortunately, not all those ideas were abandoned, at least not always and not by everyone. For the last few hundred years, you'd think that the need for war would have been diminished, as the Industrial Revolution made wealth more widespread and easy to create.

Nonetheless, it seems we have retained the same old reasons for war that we have always had, in addition to new political and religious demands. The hope for civilization is that we would now see that the cost of war actually far outweighs any benefit. Vietnam seemed to be a good example where the cost far outweighed any benefit.

In 1967, the country was still holding predominantly to the belief that the military was the good guy and our government sincerely wanted to protect America from the spread of communism. This was ably presented by the domino theory. The chaotic year 1968 changed most of that. The military came out of that badly, for American deaths and wounded increased far past what was acceptable, especially considering that we were not winning the war and had no real prospects of winning. It had become our longest, costliest, and deadliest war in recent memory. And the damage being inflicted on Vietnam became more and more dreadful, unfair, and noticeable.

Today in war or conflict, there are actions that simply should never be considered just, moral, or correct. You'd think, for example, that destroying massive amounts of land pervasively and indiscriminately with poisons would not be considered legal, moral, or allowed. Wounding and killing civilians would not be considered legal, moral, or allowed. Cratering the landscape with bombs so that it resembles the moon would not be considered legal, moral, or allowed. Burning villages and relocating peasant farmers would not be considered legal, moral, or allowed. You'd think that none of those things would be considered legal, moral, or allowed. Yet they were all employed during the Vietnam War.

I personally resolved my morality question by saying that the United States must have had good reason to risk so many men and expend so much cost. Initially, the reasoning must have been just and correct. Because of that, I could go in good conscious and do what had to be done to protect my country. Once in Vietnam, there were people trying to kill me, and therefore it was just and correct to protect my friends and myself. I could consider it "moral" at that time.

I determined that morality is an individual thing. What is allowable as moral is determined by each individual based on his own circumstances, experiences, knowledge, and history. With that, I decided I had acted morally, given the conditions, circumstances, reasoning, and what I knew at the time. I could then move on and live the rest of my life without concern. I was able to do that for the longest time.

However, with the passage of time and having gained some historical knowledge and some knowledge of government, business, leadership, and society, I have begun to have my doubts. I am no longer sure that there was a good, just, and valid moral reason for beginning that war. There certainly was not a good reason for extending it so long.

The observation that the government military-industrial complex, as President Eisenhower warned about, needed to be watched seemed to have been truer than even he could have ever imagined. Is it cynical to think it possible that politicians or the military would contrive a fake situation so that we'd have a reason to enter a war? Is it cynical to think that politicians might leave troops in harm's way in order to assure their reelection? Is it cynical to think that politicians might continue a war because their friends in business are making big money while the government pays for the war with citizen tax money?

When the war began, there was (according to many) a valid, just, and correct moral reason for it—to block the spread of communism in Southeast Asia. Most Americans do not favor living under a totalitarian dictatorship. Later, however, it seems to have become a cash cow to business friends of government politicians, bureaucrats, and presidents who somehow couldn't negotiate an early end to the war, either with or without honor. All that time spent trying to negotiate an "early end with honor" meant more lives lost, more families destroyed, and more damage to Vietnam, along with more money for the military-industrial complex and more political contributions to politicians.

In my opinion, my participation and the participation of hundreds of thousands of other people in the Vietnam War was justified for each of us because our government had convinced us that it was just, correct, and in our best national security interests. However, just to make sure we agreed with them, participation was mandated by the draft.

Regardless, the turbulent year 1968 along with the disclosure of historical truths ever since have changed many minds to thinking that the war had morphed into an unending disaster of wasted money, wasted resources, wasted lives, wasted families, and wasted Vietnamese lives in an orgy of high government corruption, greed, and lies.

Several years ago, a Marine Corps friend who had gotten into the travel business contacted me. He and some associates had started a company that led tours back to Vietnam, mostly for veterans who had been there during the war. He promised to research their units, their battles, and the locations. Then he would lead the tour to those exact locations so the vets could find some kind of closure. The forgiving and friendly Vietnamese people warmly accepted American tourism.

At first, it seemed a rewarding trip for closure, and I was very interested in going. But then I saw some pictures he had taken on one of his tours in the areas near where I had been. I saw paved roads, fences, telephone poles with wires, and buildings. It looked a lot like Minnesota or Wisconsin, except with different trees. What a strange feeling … I was sad that I saw the "improvements."

I was not sad that the people had raised their standard of living. I was sad because the innocence and beauty of an earlier time had been replaced by modernity. I really wanted to cry for the loss, and at the same time, I felt so guilty for wanting the people and things to have remained the same as they had been. Therefore, I said, "No, I can't go."

Now I sip the wine and listen to the music. The headset is no longer attached to a transistor radio. I can listen through the air to anything I want via Ethernet or Bluetooth.

I trip out, much as I did at CAP III, and think about possible travels back to Vietnam. I imagine one day riding one of those modern mopeds from An Hoa to Hoi An on a paved road right through Arizona Territory, past Go Noi Island and all those memories. I'll remember the terror of those places. I envision crossing over a new Liberty Bridge and seeing Hill 55 again. I will wheel past the places where so many had been killed or wounded, with so many memories of the beast and still so many memories of the beauty.

I can visualize cruising north from Hoi An along a palm tree–lined boulevard toward a new, modern, shiny, and sparkling Da Nang filled with new tall buildings. I will see sidewalks, picnic tables, and the miles of sandy beaches all along the way. The entire ride will be made watching blue waves crash on the white Da Nang beaches.

I see a ride to Marble Mountain and a stop to visit the holy place and perhaps to say a prayer to the people and country of Vietnam. If I can ever apologize to them for my part in this, this will be where I will do it. I am so sorry for the pain and suffering that we caused and that I may have caused.

My imaginary road trip will have us ride up the winding Highway 1 to Hai Van Pass, past the old army base with beautiful vistas to both Da Nang and Lang Co. I will come down the twisting road and pass the desolated and forgotten old French fort where I had groveled for chili from an army private. I will always remember the operation out of that old French fort, where Third Platoon was blown up, with Maddy, Lieutenant Ruggles, and the squad decimated.

I'll look forward to seeing Lang Co once again, with a possible stay at one of the new resorts there. On a day hike, I might even find that very hill where I sat and watched the tides come in and go out of the lagoon, all the while listening to my radio playing "Love Is Blue." I'll revisit where the marine blasted a hole in himself with a 3.5-inch rocket launcher on a low tide beach.

The ride will continue up Highway 1 to Phu Bai, passing the many bridges where we encountered our typhoon and where Cronen and the squad stepped on a Bouncing Betty booby trap in the railroad tunnel, which killed one and tore the legs off Hencke. Hencke deserves to be on the wall but simply is not there because he rotated home before he took his own life. I'll whisk past Claymore Pass, where Jenkins "shot the moon" and I thought he had hit it.

I see reaching Phu Bai, the end of my ride back through time. It will be a look back at a time that can't be changed but perhaps can be forgiven. Perhaps we can forgive the enemy and ourselves and forget the horrible things that happened. Perhaps we can understand that we participated in what started out as a noble, just, and valid cause that became an out-of-control, immoral, runaway military-industrial and governmental complex lust for money and power.

As I wrap up my journey back in time, I have to say that, in hindsight, it was really a miraculous time for me. I grew philosophically and became confident in my abilities to handle stress. I grew from a kid into an adult. I learned about friendship, love, difficulties, danger, deprivation, and loss. I could not have done that without the USMC and my experiences in it. I could not have done it without my friends (not just acquaintances) in it. Sergeant Taylor from back in MCRD boot camp was wrong; you couldn't and didn't just make acquaintances. You *did* make friends, lasting friends. You couldn't help it. I have nothing but respect, admiration, and love for my friends from that time.

The guys I served with were all American kids from different walks of life, backgrounds, races, and educational experiences. The common element among them all was their humanity, bravery, and willingness to risk their lives to help one another. We were all thrown into a common boiling cauldron, and to get out, we had to work together.

Officers and grunts were all just a bunch of guys doing their jobs, taking their chances, and hoping to go home. I could not be prouder to have served at that time, in that place, with those guys—heroes all.

Just one of the many beautiful sights in Vietnam

GLOSSARY

0311: This MOS signifies a Marine Corps rifleman, a grunt. Other infantry MOSs might be "0331"—machine gunner, "0341"—rockets and flamethrower, or "0351"—mortars.

actual: This represents or means the commanding officer. Kilo 3 actual would be the commanding officer of Kilo Company, Third Platoon; and Kilo 6 actual would be the commanding officer of the entire Kilo Company.

arty: Short for artillery.

ARVN: Army of the Republic of Vietnam.

blooper: An M79 handgun weapon that looks like a small sawed-off shotgun that shoots grenades shaped to fit it and so named because *bloop* is the sound that best describes it when fired.

bush: The area away from cities and/or fortified fixed compounds; any area outside the wire.

C-4: A white plastic explosive that could be shaped into different configurations, more powerful than dynamite.

C rations: Individual C rations include food and accessories, such as toilet paper. They came in a cardboard box containing items sealed in a can, and each meal had a fruit, meat, and dessert. To open the cans you needed a P-38 "John Wayne" can opener.

CAP unit: Combined Action Program. Usually a squad of marines and a platoon of ARVN or PF protecting a village.

Charlie: Common slang term for VC or NVA.

clusterfuck: To form a group in close proximity to each other, making an inviting and easy target.

CO: Commanding officer.

CP: Command post. This can be considered anything from a battalion headquarters down to a small traveling unit such as a company or even a platoon, wherever the commanding officer happens to be located.

CPL: Corporal.

deck: The ground or floor.

DI: Boot camp drill instructor.

doc: A navy corpsman assigned to a USMC infantry company.

dog tags:	Identifying information hung on a chain around the neck.
flare:	A handheld illumination device that could be triggered and sent into the air with different colors. Red usually means "bad, warning, or enemy." Green usually means "okay or good guys." White usually lights up an area, usually for landing a helicopter.
FNG:	Fucking new guy.
frag:	Fragmentation grenade.
Get some:	A term probably unique to members of the Third Battalion, Fifth Marines, which means something like "I hope you devastate all them out there" when said in conjunction with an artillery barrage or a Phantom F-104 jet bombing run on suspected enemy placements.
grunt:	An infantryman, usually dirty, sweaty, and smelly, carrying a heavy load of gear.
gun:	A 60 mm machine gun, often called a pig or hog.
head:	The bathroom (showers, toilets, sinks, and so forth).
hump:	To carry or bear a heavy load while hiking across terrain.
increment:	A small C-4 patch of explosive that could be attached to a mortar round to provide additional distance to the normal flight path.
John Wayne:	A can opener for C rations cans of food, usually kept on a chain with your dog tags.
LAAW:	Light antitank assault weapon, a rocket-propelled grenade. This is quite a bit lighter and nearly as powerful as the 3.5-inch rocket launcher (Super Bazooka).
LCPL:	Lance Corporal
LT:	Lieutenant.
medevac:	Medical evacuation, usually by helicopter.
mortar:	A 60 mm or 81 mm diameter tube with a firing pin at the bottom. A motor round is dropped down the tube and detonates a propellant that sends the charge in a parabola-shaped flight path to the enemy.
MOS:	Military operations specialty—job description.
NVA:	Short for North Vietnamese Army.
P-38:	A can opener for C rations cans of food, usually kept on a chain with your dog tags.
PF:	Popular Forces. Usually a group of locals from the village assigned to help protect the village from the VC or NVA.

point:	The person, squad, or platoon leading the patrol or sweep responsible for finding the route, the destination, and for avoiding ambushes and booby traps.
poncho:	A rain jacket with hood used when rainy or as half of a pup tent–type shelter. It usually comes with a poncho liner that is a lightweight blanket.
puff:	An AC-47 aircraft loaded with miniguns on the left side so that the plane could bank left, circling the enemy, and rain down an incredibly intense stream of fire.
RPG:	Rocket-propelled grenade.
saddle up:	"Pick up the gear and put on the backpacks. We're moving out."
skate:	To coast and have it easy, to not work hard, or to miss the worst of it.
short:	This usually means there is only a "short" time remaining in country for this person. He would be called a "short-timer."
VC:	Short for Vietcong, the South Vietnamese Communists who resisted the American-supported South Vietnamese government and American troops.
ville:	Village.
wasted:	This usually means a dead enemy but could also mean that a guy is drunk and unable to perform any duties.
wire:	The perimeter around a compound or a traveling unit such as a company or platoon. It may or may not be an actual barrier from a fortified wall or reinforced fence to a series of trip wires and flares to a simple barbed wire fence.

General Military Organization Structure

fire team:	Two to four soldiers, usually commanded by a lance corporal or corporal.
squad:	Four to ten soldiers, usually commanded by a corporal, sergeant, or staff sergeant.
platoon:	Sixteen to forty soldiers, usually commanded by a lieutenant.
company:	One hundred to two hundred soldiers, in three to five platoons, usually commanded by a captain or a major.
battalion:	Four to six companies, usually commanded by a lieutenant colonel.

ABOUT THE AUTHOR

Over a lifetime, the author has earned a BA degree in biometry from the University of Minnesota, a BS degree in computer science at National University in San Diego, and an AA degree in accounting at Mesa College, San Diego. He has earned a lifetime teaching credential in computer science for community colleges in California and has received a wealth of diverse business applications training while working for IBM, which he used while instructing a systems analysis class at Mesa College.

He has worked as a computer salesman, a hotel night auditor, a business applications computer programmer, a business computer consultant/analyst, and owner of a cloud-based business computer service bureau that hosts multiple clients and their software systems, acting as their IT departments.

Along the way, he earned a commercial pilot license and flight instructor certificate for single and multiengine airplanes with instrument ratings. That led to forty years of part-time flight instruction and owning a Part 135 on-demand airline. In the capacity as owner-operator, he acted as chief pilot and FAA-designated check airman as well as being a line pilot when required.

His experience in the marines covered the years 1967 through 1969. His Vietnam experience was from December 2, 1967, through December 20, 1968, the tumultuous year of the Tet Offensive and civil unrest in the United States. During his thirteen months, he was an infantry grunt, with training and combat experience in machine guns, mortars, rockets, and flamethrowers. He considers all life experiences valuable but evaluates his time with the marines as being the most influential on who he has become and how he conducts himself.

Printed in the United States
by Baker & Taylor Publisher Services